576147-0-20

10/75

**Residential Mobility and
Home Purchase**

Lexington Books Regional Science Monograph Series
Stan Czamanski, Editor

Stan Czamanski, *Regional and Interregional Social Accounting*

Daniel R. Fredland, *Residential Mobility and Home Purchase*

Residential Mobility and Home Purchase

A Longitudinal Perspective on the Family Life Cycle and the Housing Market

Daniel R. Fredland
The Florida State University

Lexington Books
D.C. Heath and Company
Lexington, Massachusetts
Toronto   London

Library of Congress Cataloging in Publication Data

Fredland, Daniel R.
  Residential mobility and home purchase.

  Bibliography: p.
  1. Residential mobility. 2. Residential mobility–Philadelphia metropolitan area. 3. Home ownership. I. Title.
HD7287.5.F72   301.32'6   73-11652
ISBN 0-669-89458-3

To
I.F.

Contents

List of Figures

List of Tables

Foreword

The Regional Science Monograph Series of Lexington Books, D.C. Heath and Company, is intended as a vehicle for making recent contributions in the field available to scholars, students, and practitioners. The growing impact of mathematical reasoning and the spreading use of quantitative methods in the study of spatial phenomena makes the dissemination of results of quality research all the more important.

The majority of the studies published over the past four years have dealt with intrametropolitan location of activities and with the manifold aspects of the resulting transportation problems. Professor Fredland's book attacks a closely related topic of currently great importance. Housing and the mobility of urban households stands at the center of a number of issues often loosely referred to as the urban crisis. The highly complex phenomena involved have been studied with the help of tools forged in a number of disciplines, but we are still far from a satisfactory theory of the behavior of the main decision makers. Without such a theory, explanations of urban structure, of spatial organization of urban functions, of urban blight and sprawl, of the flight to the suburbs, or of urban social decay amount to little more than a cataloguing of observed regularities.

The present volume does not claim to solve the involved problem of motivation and decision-making processes of households in their quest for shelter, but it does provide some new insights. Even more interesting is the original application of statistical tools, especially a modified version of discriminant analysis, to the study of urban phenomena. Because of both its findings and the methods of analysis employed, the volume richly deserves to be read by anyone concerned with housing and evolution of cities.

Stan Czamanski

Preface

This book did not start out to be a life-cycle study. In a Zen-like fashion it just developed into one. Originally I intended to examine residential mobility as an element in the problem of modeling urban development patterns, and also to test some propositions implied by urban land rent theory; the latter underlies many urban development modeling efforts. The best single predictor of mobility, however, is tenure—i.e., whether a family owns or rents its home; the question of how and why it came to own or rent, therefore, becomes virtually inescapable. That led to one extension of the investigation. The intimate relationship of the family life cycle to residential mobility and the purchase-rental decision then completed the definition of the scope of the present study.

The original motivation of the study led to extended consideration of the influence of job changes within the urban community on local—i.e., nonmigratory—residential movement. A clear implication of urban land rent theory and related conceptualizations of urban form is that the residential location is chosen with reference to job location. If so, one might infer that household heads who changed jobs would on that account have higher residential mobility. If this is true, land rent theory and the many applied models based on it would be further validated.

An effect of this nature was found, but it tends to be weak and delayed. These conclusions are consonant with those of other investigators. This investigation, however, like much of the earlier research on local residential mobility, is based on Philadelphia area data. Recent research on the San Francisco Bay Area has shown a much stronger tie between local residential movement and job change. Thus the subject is far from closed, and the desirability of comparative studies in other urban communities is clearly indicated.

The statistical model employed, the linear probability function, has been used only rarely in urban studies. It is a derivative of linear discriminant analysis, but lends itself better than does discriminant analysis to heuristic interpretation. It is hoped that this book demonstrates its potential utility and validity for studying urban functioning and problems. Two ad hoc tests of the performance of the equations generated from the data were devised to allay my own doubts concerning validity. These tests are presented in the text.

In carrying out this study I have had the benefit of considerable advice and other assistance from several people and organizations, the most significant of which are listed here. The suggestions of John F. Kain throughout the formative stages of this project have been invaluable. Also, the study could not have been undertaken without the data contained in the Supplemental Home Interview, performed by the Penn Jersey Transportation Study. The successor agency to Penn Jersey, the Delaware Valley Regional Planning Commission, has made the data and supporting documentation available without restriction.

Stan Czamanski, H. James Brown, S. Swami, Peter Rogers, James Frank, Andrew Dzurik, and Thomas Watts reviewed drafts of all or parts of this book and made many valuable suggestions. Henry Bruck and Albert Chevan, the two individuals responsible for the Supplemental Home Interview, gave generously of their time and insight in suggesting methods of data manipulation and in explaining obscure points of documentation.

Paul O'Brien, formerly of the Harvard Computer Center, and Robert Kolar, one of my students at Florida State University, gave crucial assistance in programming. Computation costs were defrayed through the generosity of the National Bureau of Economic Research and the Florida State University Computer Center. The maps were prepared by Langdon A. Kellogg, also a student at Florida State. Betty Willard is foremost among many secretaries who have contended valiantly with incredible handwriting and numerous "last" changes in the manuscript.

I, of course, take full responsibility for the contents of this book, particularly for any omissions or errors it may contain.

Daniel R. Fredland
Tallahassee, Florida

1

Introduction: The Symbiosis of Mobility and Housing

Each year, for the last several years, approximately 20 percent of the population in the United States has changed residence. Approximately 13 percent moved within a county, and 7 percent moved across county lines. The variation from year to year is small. Shryock reports the range for all mobility, for the years 1947-48 through 1960-61, was 18.6 to 21.0 percent. For the same period, the range for intracounty movement was 12.2 to 13.9 percent.[1] In recent years these figures have tended to remain stable.

Mobility rates are similar between metropolitan and nonmetropolitan areas. For the period 1953-54 through 1957-58, each year an average of 19.3 percent of the population of standard metropolitan areas moved, 13.5 percent between counties.[2] The comparable figures for nonmetropolitan areas were 20.0 and 12.6 percent.

Residential movement traditionally has been divided into two categories: local movement—movement within a community or urban area—and intercommunity migration. The latter typically involves changing job and social ties to friends and organizations. Local movement, occurring within a community, does not coincide with a reorientation of such a radical nature. That is the focus of this study.

Type of tenure, whether one owns or rents his dwelling, is intimately bound up with local residential movement. Owners have been found consistently to move less than renters. Changes in tenure, on the other hand, are made only in conjunction with a move. Both tenure and moving are closely related not only to each other, but also to the family life cycle—the chain of events from marriage through dissolution and death. Thus, it is necessary to study the two together.

Residential movement and tenure choice have a profound effect upon the housing market.[3] Only movers (including newly formed households) are active demanders of housing. By the same token, a large part of the housing which is available in the market consists of units vacated by movers. Maisel[4] has shown that examining the housing demand of movers, as contrasted to the predominantly static demand of the entire population, can shed considerable light on the housing market, and it greatly alters forecasts of the overall demand for rental and ownership housing.

A similar concern is the relationship of residential movement to predictive models of urban growth and form. In some cases, a forecast of the number of movers is seen as a necessary step in the overall model.[5] That is, the locational models do not depict an equilibrium distribution of the entire population, but

1

work with the mobile sector of the population. The latter includes inmigrants and newly formed families, as well as movers.

Residential movement is also of interest in relation to urban land rent theory. A usual assumption of land rent theory is that job location strongly influences the choice of residential location.[6] The choice of location is hypothesized to involve a tradeoff between land or space cost and convenient access to the place of work. If that is true, job movement should be an inducement to residential movement. A change in job location will alter the terms of the tradeoff. Consequently, the residential location chosen in relation to the old job would be suboptimal.[a] With a small job move, the degree of suboptimality may be too small to justify the cost and trouble of moving. With a longer job move, however, a residential move should allow on average a greater gain. If job moves tend to be associated to a significant degree with residential moves, and if the degree of association increases significantly with the distance of the job move, that would tend to support the hypothesis that job location influences residential location. (It is still necessary to assume the direction of causality.)

This book presents an investigation of local residential movement and tenure choice. The investigation touches upon the relationship of these two things to each other and to family characteristics, family life cycle, and to the career of the head of the household. It includes a review of past research (Chapter 2), a theoretical, or heuristic, model (Chapter 3), and an empirical investigation (Chapters 4 through 7).

The empirical investigation makes use of a survey conducted in 1960 by the Penn Jersey Transportation Study.[b] The Supplemental Home Interview (SHI), as it was known, recorded residential and related histories of approximately 6,000 families living in the Philadelphia, Pennsylvania, and Trenton, New Jersey, Standard Metropolitan Statistical Areas.

The statistical model employed in this study is a linear probability model. It is a linear function, similar to ordinary least squares linear regression, but with the dependent variable representing the probability of an event—moving or home purchase in the present case. The method is equivalent to the more venerable discriminant analysis. In the latter, the problem is to classify observations into two (or more) naturally existing groups.

---

[a]It is possible that a job move is approximately along a line connecting residence and relevant peak of the rent surface, so that any residential move after the job move would still involve negative substitution between commuting costs and land costs. It would be most extraordinary, however, if after the job move, which changes income net of commuting costs, the individual's or family's substitution surface of accessibility, space, and land cost were tangential to the market-dictated surface at his prior residential location. If residential movement were costless, there would be a change of residential location.

[b]The Penn Jersey Transportation Study was an interstate organization charged with making a long-term transportation plan for the SMSA's of Philadelphia and of Trenton, New Jersey. The survey, part of their research, was not used to any great extent by the organization. The successor agency to Penn Jersey, the Delaware Valley Regional Planning Commission, has been kind enough to make the data available.

These two methodologies have been little used in urban problem analysis or urban and regional studies. The major exception is the problem of modal split or modal choice in urban transportation. Yet many more problems can readily and profitably be construed as problems in two-way classification or probability. The present study is a case in point. Also in the housing area is the problem of housing abandonment. Using detailed census returns, one could find a great deal of information about individual housing units existing a few years ago. A linear probability model could then be used to test the influence of various unit and neighborhood characteristics on the probability of abandonment. If, from a societal point of view, abandonment appears to be excessive, too scattered, or otherwise unsatisfactory, the effectiveness of policies suggested for discouraging it or encouraging it at specific locations could then be estimated.

Another example—conceptually and statistically similar although in a fundamentally different area—is that of screening applicants for social-service programs with limited enrollment capacity. Job training programs fall into this category. The problem is to separate candidates into probable successes and probable failures. A reliable classification would increase the effectiveness of the programs while avoiding the discouraging experience of failure for unlikely candidates.[7] Also, by identifying characteristics of persons who are poorly suited for job training, such research might help to define a group requiring other kinds of public programs and services.

The method is no more difficult to apply than linear regression. Indeed, computer programs for regression can be used without modification for linear probability computation. Standard programs are also available for discriminant analysis. It is hoped that this study will serve as a demonstration of the effectiveness of these methods and thereby encourage their use for research on urban and regional problems.

2

Perspectives on Mobility and Home Purchase: A Review of the Literature

Residential Mobility

Residential mobility has long been of interest to urban planners, sociologists, economists, and geographers, and much is known about both intercommunity migration and local movement. The literature contains some overlap between the two types of mobility, and it is not always possible in reviewing past research to make a clear separation. Emphasis will be given here, however, to local, or intracommunity, movement.

Reasons connected with career and job lie behind most migration, but such reasons are rarely felt to be crucial by local movers. The difference was shown clearly in a survey conducted by Melville Branch in 1942. Of the respondents who had recently made intercity moves, 56 percent stated that they moved because of new employment, a job transfer, or to seek work. An additional 8 percent moved to be closer to work, and 3 percent were seasonal workers. Only 10 percent of recent intracity movers, however, stated that they moved to be closer to work. Most intracity movers gave reasons connected with housing for the move. Specific reasons mentioned most often were housing quality considerations, cost and size of housing, desire to own, and loss of tenure (i.e., being forced to move).[1]

Shryock and Larmon, using data from a Bureau of Labor Statistics survey, found a similar difference in motivation between migrants and local movers. Job-related reasons were given by 12 percent of "short-distance" movers, but by 62 percent of migrants.[2] (The survey covered male noninstitutional population aged 18 to 64, inclusive, in March, 1963.) A sample of families of college students, surveyed by Whitney and Brigg, gave "economic" reasons—to seek a better job or accept a job advancement—for 90 percent of their long moves. They gave such reasons for virtually none of the moves within county lines.[3] Goldstein and Mayer found a close correlation between length of move and proportion of movers who changed jobs.[4] Foote et al. cite similar findings.[5]

Not only are job-related motives exceptional in intracommunity moving, but there are a number of people who appear to move uphill from their jobs in relation to the rent surface hypothesized by land rent theory. Goldstein and Mayer found that, of those moving to Providence from the suburban ring between 1955 and 1960, 17 percent worked in the ring in 1960. Of those moving to Providence from the "outlying area" (the part of Rhode Island beyond the census-designated suburbs), 28 percent worked in the "outlying area" in 1960. There were also inmigrants to suburban municipalities from beyond the SMSA who, in 1960, worked in the "outlying area."[6]

A large proportion of residential movement is for a short distance. Goldstein and Mayer found that many movers go from one suburban residence to another or move between two residences within the central city.[7] In other studies, a significant proportion of movers have been observed to stay within the same neighborhood[8] or "section" of a city.[9] (The latter was defined as a commonly recognized part of the city.)

A recent study of residential mobility offers some contradictory evidence of the importance of job changes for residential moves. Brown and Kain[10] found in a study of the San Francisco Bay Area that local residential mobility is significantly higher at or about the time of a job change than it is without a job change. This conclusion holds true even when the comparison is controlled for a number of other influential factors, e.g., age of head of household and type of tenure. Furthermore, longer job moves, those crossing study-zone boundaries, are followed by higher residential moving rates than job changes wthin zones. Thus the question of the influence of job changes on residential mobility remains open.

Life Cycle Hypothesis

An explanation of local moving that is consistent both with the high proportion of short moves, and with the unimportance of job-related reasons for moving, is the life cycle hypothesis. The hypothesis, as advanced by Rossi and Chevan, is that housing demands change systematically with the life cycle of the family, and that moving is primarily a means of bringing demand and supply into agreement.[11]

Rossi, in conducting his initial survey, focused his attention on moving intentions. He found that the desire to move was a function of family size, age of head, tenure and tenure preference, the number of rooms in the current dwelling, and—more important—attitude towards that amount of space. Larger and younger families showed stronger mobility inclinations. The age relationship held for owners and renters, size for renters. Rossi reasoned, quite plausibly, that, with large family size, renters are more likely than owners to feel a space pinch.[12] Room count had an effect independent of size of family, but attitude about space adequacy or inadequacy had a greater effect. Opinion about what is a desirable amount of space and demand for space appear to vary among families of the same size.

Renters, in general, had a greater inclination to move than owners. Mobility inclinations were highest among renters who desired to own.

Complaints about the physical and social environment of the neighborhood were also associated with the desire to move. Convenience of location relative to work, shopping, and churches did not have as large an influence as any of the other considerations mentioned.

In a follow-up survey eight months later, Rossi did find a close correlation between previously indicated inclination to move and actual moving performance. Of those "anxious to stay," 4 percent moved; of those "anxious to move," 33 percent. Those with intermediate attitudes had intermediate proportions of movers.

Among the reasons given for moving by recent movers, Rossi found space complaints far more frequent than any other. Such complaints, furthermore, were twice as common for families that had had an increase in family size as for other families. Altogether, 45 percent of the recent movers gave space problems as an important reason for moving. The next largest category of important reasons was neighborhood complaints, but only 14 percent of the movers gave answers in that category. That category was more common among families which previously had owned their own home. Cost complaints—the next category, with 12 percent—were more frequent among former renters.

Space considerations were also most important among the criteria for the choice of a new dwelling. In regard to choice of neighborhood, locational convenience was most important. It was mentioned by 26 percent of the movers, as against 6 percent who mentioned social composition of the neighborhood. Thus, locational convenience was more frequently relevant to the choice of new residence than it was to the decision to move from the old residence.

Rossi's work went far towards substantiating the life cycle hypothesis. It also gives reason to believe that locational considerations are generally not crucial in the decision to move. The usefulness of his work, however, is seriously flawed by heavy reliance on attitudinal data and by dissimilar coverage of movers and nonmovers.

Attitudinal data are highly subject to memory problems. Reasons for past actions may be forgotten soon after the event. A related problem is that some factors which are implicitly controlling may be taken for granted and not consciously considered. The distance between a new residence and the householder's job could be one such factor.

Rossi's postfacto data on movers is not matched by similar data on nonmovers. The omission causes uncertainty about the actual effect of factors hypothesized to affect mobility. For example, Rossi states that the birth of a child preceding the move was correlated with a certain difference in the reasons given for moving. But he says nothing about nonmovers who had children in the same period. It would be relevant to ask if all families which experienced the birth of a child had a significantly greater probability of moving than other families.

Chevan was able to rectify these shortcomings in Rossi's work. His dependent variable is "moves per hundred years of exposure," not moving intentions. His independent variables represent family charcteristics and events hypothesized to affect moving. His conclusions do not depend on attitudinal data, and he gives little attention to such data.

Chevan's work further substantiates the life cycle hypothesis. Chevan gives primary attention to moving by families with married heads. Marriage, itself, was strongly associated with moving. Chevan found that 69 percent of grooms moved within three months either side of marriage.[a] Length of time married and birth of children were also significant. The proportion of families moving declined with time married. For any length of time married, however, it was greater in periods when a child was born.[b]

A move in the previous three-year period of observation is, in the case of owners, associated with lower moving propensities. That is not true for renters. Families appear to anticipate changes in their own housing demands when they buy a home, but not when they rent.[13]

The ratio of persons per room is positively associated with propensity to move. For any given ratio at the start of the period, the birth of a child causes a higher propensity to move. The departure of a child is also associated with higher moving rates, but the effect is less than that of a birth.

Movers tend through the first 24 years of marriage to increase the number of rooms, but, afterward, to reduce them. The decline in the proportion of movers with time married, however, allows the number of persons per room for all families to decline steadily after 18 years of marriage.[14]

Chevan also examined moves after dissolution of marriage. He found that 10 percent of surviving spouses moved in the first year after death of the other. The structure of the survey, however, is such that people leaving the region were not recorded. Furthermore, women who remarry and survivors of either sex moving in with relatives or to institutions would be lost to the survey. These gaps in coverage seriously compromise the findings.

Movement data for the divorced and separated is similarly flawed. Chevan found that 20 percent moved at separation, 23 percent at divorce. But at least 50 percent of the marriage partners must have moved at either of those events. Evidently, a large proportion remarried, left the region, or gave up being heads of households. There may also be response error. In any event, the survey is unreliable in regard to movement immediately after family dissolution.[c]

Leaving aside movement at the time of change in marital status, however,

[a]The Penn Jersey Supplemental Home Interview, the data source for Chevan's work, recorded the movement only of heads of household. It excluded, therefore, the moves by wives prior to marriage.

[b]The time variable was handled by grouping families by time married. Three-year periods were used for those married 18 years or less. Each three-year period for each family was treated as a separate observation. (Chevan, pp. 96-99.)

[c]That will also hold for use of the data in this thesis. Nevertheless, variables for becoming widowed, etc., are included in the statistical models so as to control for those events in estimating the effect of other factors.

Chevan was aware of these problems in the data concerning the unmarried. See Chevan, pp. 168-169 and 204-205.

Chevan's findings might give some indication of local movement by unmarried household heads. Two regularities that emerge from his examination are that movement rates decline with age and are lower for owners than for renters. In relation to these factors, the unmarried resemble the married.

There was a small number of remarried grooms in the survey. Their moving history after marriage tends to resemble that of grooms in their first marriage. The major differences are that only 39 percent moved at marriage, and there was less moving in the first six years of marriage by the remarried than by families in their first marriage.

Chevan did not examine job changes as such, but he did examine the effect of occupational mobility upon married heads of household. He defined such mobility as a shift from one broad occupational category (e.g., upper white collar) to another. In general, any change was associated with higher rates of moving. This is especially true during the first 12 years of marriage.

Status at the beginning of the three-year observation period and direction of job mobility make a difference. Those beginning as "lower white collar" workers tended to move more with downward occupational shift, and to move less with upward, than they did with no change in occupational category.[d] One can speculate that that group tended to anticipate upward mobility in selection of residence. If a rise in status failed to occur, they tended to move somewhat more than if it had. If a decline occurred, they moved much more.

Retirement also affected movement. Those who retired moved somewhat more than those who continued to work or who were already retired at the start of an observation period.

Chevan's technique resembles an analysis of variance. (No tests of significance, however, were made.) He partitioned the sample by up to four independent variables at once and compared the weighted mean moving rates for the cells. (The weights were the number of families represented by each observation.) Generally, two of the controlling variables were marital status[e] and duration of that status. The remaining two could represent conditions at a point in time, such as size of family or persons per room, or changes, such as job mobility or birth of a child or children.

For both married and unmarried, one uniformity stands out. Almost regardless of the value of other variables, mobility declines with time. For example, at any given number of years of marriage, those who had a child born moved more frequently during the period than those who did not. But, considering either those who did or did not have a child in an observation period, rates of moving declined with increasing length of time married.

---

[d]The occupational groupings used by Chevan are, in the implied status order: upper white collar, lower white collar, upper blue collar, and lower blue collar (Chevan, pp. 91-96).

[e]The marital-status distinction was handled by categorizing families according to the head's marital status and then discussing one category at a time. Each tabulation contains data for one marital-status category and has up to three additional controlling variables.

Families simply become more settled. Exceptions are rare, the principal one being in regard to tenure.[f]

The question still remains, however, of why time is so closely correlated with mobility. Chevan examined simultaneously only a small number of variables. The omitted variables in any of his tables may change value systematically over the life cycle of a family, with the result that time is a proxy for them. The apparent influence of time may be a composite of the effect of aging itself on a person's willingness to move and of all the other factors correlated with time.

Tenure is one factor which changes value over time and which is important in relation to mobility. Chevan and others have observed that owners move less than renters.[15] Chevan also observed, in examining the behavior of married families, that half or more of the movers at any stage in the family life cycle buy their homes.[16] Thus, movement in the early years leads directly to an increased proportion of owners, and hence lower mobility, among those married longer.[g] Also, for married home owners, unless the dwelling is small (four rooms or fewer), the usual relationship between time married and mobility no longer holds. (That is the exception mentioned above.)

The fact that time married is not correlated with the mobility of home owners (except for those in small dwellings) increases the suspicion that time married gains much of its importance as a proxy. The question of proxy for what may not be completely answerable, but the research described in later chapters is designed to separate the influence of some of the factors correlated with age.

Life Style Influences

In addition to tangible influences on moving, it has been suggested that people move to realize a certain life style. Wendell Bell found that the reasons for moving expressed by a large proportion of recent movers to two Chicago suburbs showed a "familism" value orientation.[17] "Familism" is defined as valuing family life as an end in itself. Eight-one percent of Bell's respondents gave as a reason for moving that they thought the new residence would be better for children. Seventy-seven percent found life more enjoyable in the suburbs. Only 21 percent gave job-related reasons.[18] Bell suggests that the familism orientation reinforces the life cycle factors in causing people to move and in guiding choice of new residence.

Influence on social status mobility stemming from career mobility has also been found to influence residential movement. In a survey of one fairly new (six

---

[f]Owners of houses with five rooms or more have low movement rates which do not change monotonically with years of marriage (Chevan, Table 52, p. 113).

[g]Chevan noted that 60 percent of families are owners by six years of marriage. (Table 46, p. 104.)

years old) residential subdivision, Leslie and Richardson found that social mobility expectations, class differences perceived by respondents between themselves and their neighbors, education, and house attitude were highly significant in relation to actual moving and moving intentions.[19] Age, household size, and tenure type were not significantly correlated with moving.

Leslie and Richardson do not deny family life cycle is important, but they think social mobility is, also. A change of social status can induce a family to move to a residence or neighborhood which, in some way, better expresses its new status. As was seen, Chevan's work, which is later, appears to substantiate their hypothesis.

In one sense, the tenure and life style questions interact. Home ownership is highly desired by most people, and the motivations seem to include a variety of intangible reasons.[20] Rossi found, as was stated earlier, that the highest mobility inclinations were found among renters who desire to own. To the extent that ownership is desired for intangible reasons, the desire to own may be considered a life style influence.

Population Characteristics and Moving

Marital status and sex are both associated with large differences in local movement. The differences persist when the population is stratified by age (see Tables 2-1 and 2-2).

The low moving rate shown in Table 2-2 for young single people, those under 25, may be due to the status of many of them as family members. Chevan reported an annual moving rate of over 40 percent for single household heads

Table 2-1

Percent of Population Aged 14 or Over[a] Moving Within County, March, 1965–March, 1966, by Marital Status and Sex

Marital Status	Male	Female
Married	12.5	12.1
Married April 1965-March 1966	62.6	54.4
Separated	27.4	25.0
Other married–Spouse absent	22.0	17.0
Widowed	10.6	9.0
Divorced	23.8	19.4
Single	10.1	10.1

[a]As of March, 1966.

Source: U.S. Bureau of The Census, *Current Population Reports*, Series P-20, No. 156, "Mobility of the Population of the United States, March 1965-March 1966," (1966), Table 6, pp. 18-19.

Table 2-2

Percent of Population Aged 14 or Over Moving Within County, March, 1965–March, 1966, by Marital Status, Sex and Age[a]

Age	Single		Married		All Other		Total	
	M	F	M	F	M	F	M	F
14-17	9.7	9.2	n.r.	n.r.	n.r.	n.r.	9.8	10.3
18-24	9.0	11.8	40.4	34.3	40.0	32.4	20.2	24.1
25-34	15.4	17.0	21.4	16.0	35.9	27.4	21.3	17.3
35-44	16.9	9.8	15.4	9.0	39.2	20.6	17.1	10.4
45-64	8.3	6.1	9.3	5.4	27.8	11.9	11.0	6.9
65 and over	14.0	6.7	6.8	4.4	14.5	7.4	9.1	6.3
Total	10.1	10.1	12.5	12.1	19.1	13.2	12.4	11.9

[a]As of March, 1966.

n.r.: not reported.

Source: Same as Table 2-1.

that were under 25 years old.[21] Single family members move much less than single household heads.[22]

When the low moving rates of young single people are accounted for, three conclusions can be drawn from Table 2-2: the proportion of movers declines with age; men move more than women; and, after age 24, single and married people move less than others.

A number of writers discuss the relationship between income and residential mobility, but the picture that emerges is not clear-cut. Reporting on a study of Amsterdam, Netherlands, made in the 1930s, Thomas stated that out-migrants of the city included a disproportionately high number of families in the upper income groups.[23] Most of the out-migrants were going to the suburbs. Foote et al. report similar findings concerning families moving to the suburbs. They find, however, that the mean income of local movers is slightly below the general average.[24] Maisel found an inverted-U relationship between residential mobility and income.[25] Families in a "middle income" range moved more than those above or below. (Middle income covered the range $2,000-$5,999 in 1959.)

The above-average income of city-to-suburb movers is not surprising. Higher income families are attracted by the space and neighborhood amenities offered in the suburbs and by the newer, better quality housing the suburbs typically offer.

On the other hand, no direct explanation comes to mind for the overall relationship of income to mobility. Maisel suggests an indirect relationship. A disproportionately large number of families with under $2,000 income are elderly (head over 65), and an above-average proportion of those with income over $6,000 own their homes. Both age and home ownership lead to low mobility. The implication is that income has no independent effect.

In passing, it might be mentioned that location and mobility frequently have been held to be associated. Rossi differentiated parts of Philadelphia which he considered mobile and used that differentiation in structuring his sample. More recently, the *Current Population Reports* show higher mobility rates for central cities than for suburbs.[26] Whether location is actually significant for mobility, however, is undetermined. It may be that the higher mobility of certain areas is fully accounted for by such factors as family characteristics of area residents. Rossi, however, reports that all types of family had higher mobility inclinations in mobile areas than in stable areas.[27] Also, as stated above, he found complaints about neighborhood environment to be associated with mobility intentions. From this alone one might expect neighborhood characteristics to influence rates of movement.

One demographic characteristic generally considered of cardinal importance—race—was left to the end of the discussion. Nonwhites have generally been found to move more than whites. To consider the pattern for metropolitan areas throughout the country, in the year March 1965-March 1966, the intracounty mobility of nonwhites living in central cities of metropolitan areas was approximately one and one-half times that of whites (21.5 percent compared to 14.4).[28] In suburban areas, nonwhites had nearly double the intracounty mobility of whites (20.0 percent and 10.7 percent).[29] A higher proportion of whites make intercounty moves, but that difference is not enough to reverse the higher total residential mobility of nonwhites. The pattern of nonwhites having greater intracounty, and smaller intercounty, mobility is not new. It goes back, at least to the 1940s.[30]

Straits reports the mobility difference between whites and nonwhites in Chicago with somewhat greater analysis.[31] He also found that nonwhites moved more frequently than whites. Age, type of family, educational and occupational differences, migration status, and an income proxy failed to account for the difference. (Tests were made with only one or two controlling variables at a time.) Strait's conclusion is that other factors than life cycle or socioeconomic status account for racial differences in mobility. He suggests that the poorer quality and restricted choice of housing available to blacks lead to more "push" factors acting on black households, thus raising blacks' movement rates.

A more recent analysis, based on a nation-wide sample, has found black mobility not to be higher if the comparison is controlled by tenure status.[32] Black renters were found to move less than white, black owners more. Overall, when controlled for tenure, black mobility was lower. The reasons given by blacks for moving tended more often to reflect forced moves—for example, eviction or dwelling unit destruction or demolition. This bears out Strait's speculations. It is also consistent with the higher proportion of renters among black households and the poorer average quality of housing occupied by blacks.

The whole question of race and residential movement becomes even more involved when the questions of segregation and racial succession are considered. Not only are housing opportunities for blacks involved, but also the effect of neighborhood racial change on white mobility rates. This topic has an extensive literature, but it, along with most of other neighborhood effects, is beyond the scope of the present study.[33]

Choice of Tenure

Residential tenure has been studied generally in one of two ways. The more traditional is to examine the relationship of tenure to demographic characteristics and income for the entire population considered in cross-section. The cross-sectional approach leads to some anomalies. The problems are the result of families' remaining in dwellings after the circumstances which influenced their choice of dwelling have changed. The alternative, the marginal approach, is to consider the propensity of families with varied characteristics to buy a home.

Both approaches—cross-sectional and marginal—are represented in the short study, previously cited, by Maisel. In the first part of the article, Maisel discusses some aspects of the housing consumption by families of varied characteristics in the Los Angeles SMSA in 1960. Among other things, the propensity for home ownership, by income, is shown for all households and for households that had moved in the period 1958-1960. In both cases, income and home ownership are positively correlated. For all families, however, the percentage of home owners is nearly constant across the three lowest income groups (see Table 2-3). Furthermore, for the lowest income groups, the value of owned homes (all owners) shows virtually no income elasticity. For those who had recently moved, the proportion of home owners increases steadily with income. Few low income recent movers were buyers. The anomaly of high ownership by low-income strata, and unexpectedly high value (or number of rooms), has been observed

Table 2-3

Home Ownership Rates (%) and Value, by Income, Los Angeles SMSA, 1960

Income	Under $2000	$2000-3999	$4000-4999	$5000-5999	$6000-7999	$8000-9999	$10,000-and over
All families	37	36	40	50	63	71	79
Recent movers	15	15	20	29	41	49	60
Median value of home, All owners	$12,850	$13,450	$13,628	$14,050	$14,925	$16,040	$20,450

Source: Sherman J. Maisel, "Rates of Ownership, Mobility and Purchase," in *Essays in Urban Land Economics in Honor of the Sixty-Fifth Birthday of Leo Grebler* (Los Angeles: University of California, Real Estate Research Program, 1966), Tables 1 and 6.

before. Maisel and others account for it by observing that many households with elderly heads and low cash income own homes which they have occupied many years. The mortgages are paid off, and the family can afford, therefore, to continue to occupy a dwelling it could not now purchase.

It has also been observed that large families are more likely than small to own their own homes, income held constant.[34] But, many small families at all income levels own their homes. Presumably, a disproportionately large share of small, low-income, home-owning families are elderly. Older couples, most of whom are home owners, tend not to move, even when their children no longer live with them.[h]

The point of the foregoing, as made by Maisel, is that to predict or understand housing market behavior, it is necessary to look at marginal changes, not average consumption. The propensity of families to change their housing is more significant for housing market activity and housing stock changes than is the cross-sectional housing consumption pattern.

In the second part of his investigation, Maisel used another approach to examine factors influencing the propensity to own and propensity to purchase.[i] The questions were examined by means of linear discriminant functions. The chief difference between the results on owning and purchasing is in relation to age. Older heads of household are more likely to own and less likely to purchase than younger.

The effect of ownership on mobility explains the difference. Home owners are less likely to move than renters. Without moving, they cannot buy a home. If Maisel, in investigating propensity to purchase, had controlled for tenure prior to the period of observation, his results might have been substantially different.[j]

Maisel's major point, however, is well illustrated. What he calls average and marginal performance differ significantly. That is, the static propensity to own differs from the propensity to purchase.

A comparison of the work of Lee[35] and Maisel further illustrates the overwhelming effect of prior home ownership. In Maisel's analysis of purchasing, the independent variables are income, family type, age of head, and family size. All but income are represented by binary variables for various categories. Age, income, and one of the family type variables proved significant. Lee has

---

[h]Chevan states, however, that older couples, if they do move, tend "to choose a time shortly before or after children leave home." (Chevan, p. 137.)

[i]These examinations were based upon data from the 1960 U.S. Census 1:1000 tape. Data for the four largest SMSA's in the Western United States were used.

[j]Maisel also performed a discriminant analysis of the propensity to move. His results show family size and income to be significantly negatively related to moving. But both are also positively related to ownership, which is negatively related to mobility. Without ownership being considered in the analysis, it is not possible to determine the independent effect of family size and income.

In the final part of his article, where he discusses a Markov-chain model for the housing market as a whole, Maisel refers to an analysis he did of tenure choice by movers explicitly, rather than home purchase by the entire population. But he did not present those results.

performed a comparable analysis of propensity to purchase. His model includes, in addition to variables comparable to those examined by Maisel, the head of household's occupation and education, race, region within the country, "community type" (metropolitan area or not), and prior home ownership.

Only the last, prior home ownership, proved significant. Its effect was negative. The immobility of homeowners overwhelms whatever independent influence the other variables might have.

Chevan escaped the problem of the overwhelming influence of prior ownership by considering the tenure choice made by movers.[36] He examined the propensity to buy, given a move, in relation to time married, prior tenure, and race. (He considered the tenure choice only of families with a married head.)

Former owners showed a stronger propensity to buy than former renters. Seventy-two percent of former owners married up to three years bought again. From 3 through 30 years of marriage, approximately 90 percent of former owners bought and approximately 80 percent of those married over 30 years bought again upon moving. More than half of former renters also bought upon moving. Their propensity to buy, however, reached a peak of only 65 percent. The peak occurred between 13 and 15 years of marriage.

Nonwhite movers tended to buy less frequently than whites. Differences in performance by race, however, were not considered in conjunction with former tenure. Differences in prior tenure, or other measurable interracial differences, may account for the difference in propensity to buy. That cannot be determined from Chevan's data.

These separate threads were pulled together in recent analysis by Kain and Quigley.[37] Using a St. Louis sample, they examined the probability of home ownership, and of home purchase given a recent move, by means of a model similar to that employed here. Family type and size, age of head, income, race, and prior tenure were shown as significantly related to the choice of tenure by movers. Generally speaking, a white household with an older, married male head, that had owned its previous dwelling, was shown to be more likely to buy than a household with one or more contrasting characteristics. The interracial difference is attributed to discrimination in the housing market, not to any conjectural differences of taste.

Conclusion

The literature contains discussion of many factors which influence local residential mobility. Families tend to move in response to changes in size and composition. The family changes lead to altered space demand, and the families move to bring their consumption and demand into agreement. Age and home ownership, on the other hand, act in combination to inhibit moving. A high proportion of movers, at least if they are married, buy their homes. Once they have bought, their mobility is much lower. Thus, for any age cohort (defined in terms of date of birth), the proportion of home ownership rises with the passage of time, and mobility is correspondingly reduced. In addition, even for those who continue to be renters, mobility declines with age.

There are other factors, however, which may influence mobility. Life style considerations and changes in the head of household's occupational-social status have been suggested. It is also possible that change of job location and commuting considerations have an effect.

The research done to date does not include a simultaneous evaluation of the factors considered to influence mobility. It is impossible, therefore, to gauge the relative importance of the factors or to determine which factors have an independent effect and which operate as proxies. The second question is especially important in relation to age.

Home ownership and home purchase have both been examined in the literature. The examination of home ownership by the total population is somewhat unsatisfactory for understanding the housing market. The inertia of families, especially owners, causes current housing consumption to be out of equilibrium with current housing demands.

Movers may be considered the active margin of the housing market.[k] Lee and Maisel have studied one part of that margin—home purchase. The results of their investigations are, however, limited and contradictory. While there is a reasonable, if speculative, explanation of the contradiction, one is left knowing little about what influences the demand for home purchase. The recent study by Kain and Quigley is more comprehensive than Maisel's and more clear-cut and conclusive than Lee's. It tends to corroborate the findings of Maisel as well as (to anticipate) the more detailed findings in Chapter 7 of this study.

[k]In one sense, nonmovers also influence the market. They retain housing which, if they did move, would become part of the actively exchanged stock. If they were to move, they would also add to active demand. Thus any change in the propensity of any sector of the population to move would have important effects upon the housing market.[38]

3

Model of the Family Life Cycle and Housing Decisions

Of the authors discussed in the preceding chapter, only Chevan[1] considered both sides of the two-way relationship between moving and tenure. One of his statements provides a major hint for the formation of the model spelled out below. It is his observation that movers, if they go from rental to ownership, greatly reduce their prospective mobility. His examination of the factors influencing tenure choice by movers, however, is limited.

The model that follows is an attempt to account for residential mobility, tenure choice, and the relationship between them. It is the basis of the empirical research discussed in later chapters. One of the considerations affecting its form is the desire to avoid the research problems which have arisen in the attempts reported above to analyze home purchase.

The model describes moving and tenure as affecting each other in a circular way. Although moving and tenure choice are closely intertwined in practice, they are separated for purposes of analysis.

The Decision Calculus for Moving and Tenure Choice

Housing economists usually view a housing unit as a capital good that is valued for the stream of services it renders. This distinguishes it from nondurable consumer goods, which are valued for the immediate or short term pleasure they yield. (Consumer durables, such as appliances and automobiles, are an ambiguous middle category.) This view of housing—that it is a capital good—has been extended to the act of moving. Moving involves a one-time cost and is viewed as an investment.[a]

It is assumed that, when a family first occupies a dwelling unit, it chooses the unit that is the optimum available in relation to their pattern of preferences for various aspects of housing service and for other goods and services, housing market prices[b] and rents, and their budget. Events following the move that change the family's preference pattern or means will tend to make the unit less nearly optimal. When the difference between optimum and actual is great

---

[a]A similar formulation has been applied to migration. In the case of migration, the major return on the investment typically is higher earnings. For migrants beyond retirement age, however, the return must come from improved living conditions. Hence, the decision calculus of elderly migrants resembles that described below for local movers.

[b]Prices should be understood to include financing terms and other aspects of the cost of home ownership, such as taxes.

19

enough to justify the trouble and expense of moving, a move will be made. Indeed, the assumed purpose of residential movement is to adjust housing consumption to fit a family's means and desires.

Preferences may be shaped both by the current size, composition, and employment of the members of the family, and by anticipations. Because of the costs of moving, a family will, it is assumed, choose a dwelling that yields optimum satisfaction over as long a period as can be foreseen. Thus, changes in a family's situation that occur shortly after a move may make its housing more suitable in a current sense. Given the normal effects of time discount, however, changes in the factors that affect housing desires will tend to cause divergence between desired and actual housing. The exceptions would occur, generally, only during a short period following a move. For example, a couple might well make allowance for the imminent birth of a child when selecting a residence. They would be less likely to take into account the possibility of a subsequent child.

In symbols, the decision to move can be represented as follows.

Let:

$_tI$ = family income in year t.

$_tF$ = family demographic characteristics and preference patterns in t.

HUQ = housing unit quality.

HUS = housing unit size.

NQ = neighborhood quality.

LE = location relative to head of household's employment.

TS = tenure status (owner or renter).

$_tCP$ = cost parameters—e.g., interest, tax rates, insurance costs—in year t.

Then, for any housing unit, i, for any given family, the annual monetary evaluation of the satisfaction yielded can be expressed, somewhat generally, as:

$$_tS_i = S(HUQ_i, HUS_i, NQ_i, LE_i, _tF, _tI) \tag{3.1}$$

Note that the last two terms, which pertain to the family, influence the evaluation of the housing characteristics represented by the other terms in the parentheses. That is, there is interaction between family and housing characteristics within the S function.

Similarly, the costs can be expressed as:

$$_tC_i = C(HUQ_i, HUS_i, LE_i, TS_i, _tCP_i) \tag{3.2}$$

Then, the net satisfaction with a housing unit, i, in year t, $_tN_i$, becomes

$$_tN_i = _tS_i - _tC_i \tag{3.3}$$

This can be capitalized into a net present value of the act of living in a particular dwelling, $NPVL_i$, as follows:

$$NPVL_i = \sum_{t=1}^{T} \left[{_t}N_i / (1+r)^t \right] - MC_T / 1 + r)^T \qquad (3.4)$$

where T is the period for which the family contemplates remaining in that dwelling, MC_T is anticipated moving cost in year T, and r is the rate of discount applicable to future benefits and costs.[c] Note that moving costs—to be discussed below—include costs of selling an owner-occupied home.

On the basis of the foregoing, it is possible to state the conditions for a move to be made. It is that

$$NPVL_i^* - NPVL_c > MC \qquad (3.5)$$

where $NPVL_i^*$ is the time cumulation net benefit from the best alternative to the housing unit currently occupied (unit c), and MC the moving costs associated with the move to i^*. This presumes that families at appropriate times evaluate alternatives, so as to be at least roughly aware of $NPVL_i^*$. It also illustrates the critical importance of moving costs.

Once the decision to move has been made, the unit selected for a new residence is that with the highest attainable $NPVL_i^*$. It need not be assumed that the family has full information on all possible choices. Comparisons will be limited and simplified in consideration of the cost and effort required for information gathering. Even so, given the wide variation among housing choices typically available, consistent and analyzable patterns should still emerge.

In evaluating future satisfactions from housing, there are a number of sources of uncertainty. The average householder is not well equipped to make long-term predictions of neighborhood quality. Such a prediction would have to include physical condition, traffic intensity, social composition, and the quality of such neighborhood-linked services as schools. The factors of own family composition and income are also uncertain. Even if the eventual occurrence of life cycle events can be anticipated with near certainty, the timing is open to question. Furthermore, the nature of the family as extended by such events as marriage of children is unpredictable. There may or may not, for example, be frequent overnight visits by mature children and their future spouses and offspring. As for income, while the general lifetime earning curve for large groups may be predictable, considerable variation is possible between individuals and the average for their social stratum. Income, family composition, and life style, in

---

[c]The denominator of the terms on the right hand side of (3.4) is simply an expression of time discount of future net benefits or costs. It reflects the accepted generalization that future returns or costs count for less at present than do current returns or costs.

turn, affect the monetary evaluation of all the other variables in the S function.

Turning to costs, uncertainty for owners attaches to future tax rates and assessments, utility costs, and the unit cost of repair services. For renters, the cost of new construction is also a consideration, since housing rents are affected by conditions of supply. Homeowners are in large degree protected from the impact of inflation in construction costs.

The many uncertainties suggest that the discount rate for estimating the $NPVL_i$ is high as compared with, say, the rates appropriate for industrial or governmental investment decisions. Also, the uncertainties and hence the discount rate for renters should be greater than for owners. This implies that near-term demographic or career events that influence the $_tS_i$ and $_tC_i$ calculations should be highly significant for the $NPVL_i$ calculations and hence for the decision to move. Events further removed in time will diminish rapidly in significance. Near-term events, moreover, should have a greater relative effect on the mobility of renters than on owners. With a higher discount rate, future values of $_tN_i$ for large t are more heavily discounted. Also, empirically, the planning horizon, T, is shorter for renters, meaning there are fewer terms in the $NPVL_i$ summation. As a result, the measurable, short term mobility response to factors affecting current net housing satisfaction, $_tN_i$, should be greater for renters than for owners.

Finally, the moving-cost differences associated with tenure are hypothesized to have a major effect on the amount of moving. The cost of selling a home is approximately 7 percent of the capital value.[2] Home owners must add that rather substantial charge to their moving bill. This raises the threshold by which the satisfaction available from another dwelling must exceed that available from the current home. (See Equation (3.5).) There may also be a self-selection process which affects the relationship between tenure and mobility. In choosing their present tenure, families might have been guided by their expectations for future mobility. Those expecting to move again within a short period would decide to rent[d] more frequently than those anticipating stability. In Equation (3.4), it can be seen that a longer planning horizon reduces the negative effect of eventual moving costs. Hence, with long term stability in housing desires anticipated, the eventual high cost of moving from an owner-occupied dwelling has less impact on $NPVL_i$ than it would if T is short. For a family which anticipates rapidly changing desires, the denominator of $MC_T/(1+r)^T$ is small, and there is incentive to reduce MC_T. This can be done by renting rather than purchasing.

---

[d]Rental is construed, somewhat arbitrarily, to include all forms of tenure other than home ownership. It includes living rent-free and receiving lodging as part of the compensation for a job.

Structure of the Investigation

The mobility decision represented in Equation (3.5), and similarly the choice of new dwelling when moving, involve comparison of sums of discounted utility valuations less costs. The valuations and costs in turn depend on a variety of items. Any one of these items might affect the decisions. Whether or not a given influential factor is critical depends on several variables, such as the differences among the $NPVL_i$'s without that factor and on the discounted impact of that factor. Hence, the effect of any factor is stochastic, not determinate. This leads to an investigation focused on the probability of moving and of home purchase rather than on some mechanism for absolute determination.

While a whole lifetime of events and conditions can affect the $NPLV_i$'s, that much information is hardly available to the researcher. Fortunately for present purposes, the effect of the time discounting phenomenon—discussed above—is to give greater weight to current and near-future conditions and events than to influences far removed into the future. Hence a measurable relationship between events in a two year period and housing decisions can be found. Similarly, current status variables are more important than future, and a number of status variables can be related both to mobility and to tenure choice.

A choice of tenure is made with every move, and generally such a choice can be made only in conjunction with a move. Otherwise tenure is fixed. These assertions imply certain assumptions concerning the supply side of the housing market. One necessary assumption is that housing units do not move from one tenure classification to the other without a change of occupant. There are exceptions. A family might, for example, buy the house it has been renting. But such cases seem to be trivial in number and can safely be ignored. It is also necessary to assume that housing units in which a family could accommodate itself are available in each tenure category. The condition of the housing market in the study area tends to support that assumption, too. (See Appendix 3A.)

The assertion that a tenure choice can be made only in conjunction with a move leads directly to the structure of the investigation. The probability of moving is examined for all families. The probability of buying a home is examined as a contingent probability, with a move being given. Nonmovers are excluded from the second phase of the investigation.

Changes in family size and composition are hypothesized to be major causes of altered housing desires and, hence, of moving, while expectation of changes affect tenure choice of movers. Both the changes and the expectations are radically different for married and unmarried household heads. Marriage, for example, is the one marital status considered lifelong and desirable for adults, and most children are born to married couples. Furthermore, a married couple must satisfy at least two adults with any housing choice, while an unmarried person generally has no other adult to consult.

Consequently, moving performance and tenure choice when moving would tend to differ significantly between households headed by married couples and others. Separate hypotheses apply to the two groups. The discussion immediately following applies to married families. Households with unmarried heads are discussed later.

Mobility of Married Couples

The mobility of a family, measured as the probability of moving in a given time period, is hypothesized to be subject to several influences: life cycle events; demographic characteristics; job moves; changes in income and occupational status; and current housing size, location, quality, and tenure type. Some of these factors may be expected to cause a change in a family's housing desires, increasing ($NPVL_i^* - NPVL_c$), so as to increase mobility. Others may be considered to influence the cost of moving. In addition, some aspects of current housing consumption may be considered symptomatic of preexisting disequilibrium between demand and consumption, giving a low $NPVL_c$. They, too, will be associated with increased mobility.

Mobility is expected to decline rapidly with age. The rate of decline, however, almost of necessity becomes less rapid with rise in age. Mobility cannot drop below zero.

The basis for expecting a decline in mobility with age is varied. In part, it is the generally accepted observation that older people make changes of any kind less easily than younger. The attachment to familiar surroundings appears to increase with age. In effect, the psychological cost of moving becomes higher. A more concrete consideration, one which may be important for younger families, is the rapid increase in income through the early adult years.[e] As income

---

[e]The tendency of income to rise until about age 40 and then fall may be seen in cross-sectional data such as the following:

Age of Head of Spending Unit	Median Income 1959
18-24	$3,340
25-34	5,430
35-44	6,040
45-54	5,740
55-64	4,270
65 and over	1,920

Source: George Katona, Charles A. Lininger, and Richard F. Kosobud, *1962 Survey of Consumer Finances* (Ann Arbor, Michigan: Survey Research Center, Institute of Social Research, The University of Michigan, 1963), Table 1-5.

Given the constant tendency of average incomes to rise, such data probably understates the normal increases which occur for any individual before middle age and overstates the subsequent declines. For example, by the time a person aged 20 in 1959 reaches age 40, the median income for the 35-44-year-old group may be expected to exceed $6,040 (in constant dollars), the level shown for 1959. Similarly, people over 65 in 1959 were under 45 before 1939. Their median real income in the 1930s was much lower than the median for the 35-44 age group in 1959.

increases, the family can improve its housing consumption.[f] For renters, that usually requires moving. For owners, it may be more expedient to move than to alter the current home. In later years, when income is declining, often on account of retirement, there is not a strong tendency to move and adjust housing consumption downward. That may be due to a ratchet effect, to a prior decline in family size which reduced nonhousing demands on the family budget, or to the previously mentioned personal attachment to the home.

Superimposed on the effect of age, and the factors for which age may be a proxy, is the effect of family increase and decrease. Increase and decrease might both be assumed to alter a family's desire for space. While families of a given size differ in the amount of space they desire, any family is likely to want additional space with another member. The desire for space would, by the same token, decline when children mature and leave home. The greater fixity of older people also has an effect. Hence, we would expect newer families, those married up to, say, 20 years, to be experiencing the birth of children and to respond fairly frequently to the births. Families married over 20 years, on the other hand, would be experiencing diminishing size, but not responding as often to it.[g]

Regardless of change or stability in the number of people in a household, the ratio of persons per room might be important. Families with much more or much less space than the average might be expected to move. For families with average consumption preferences, a very large or small amount of space would lead to a suboptimal overall pattern of consumption.[h]

In addition, a small number of rooms is hypothesized to lead independently to decreased current satisfaction and moving. Dwellings with one or two rooms do not permit the conventional separation of functions (sleeping, cooking, social) which is possible with three rooms. If the household has three or more persons, four rooms are typically desired; that allows, in addition to separation of functions, separate bedrooms for the couple and the other member or members of the household.

The presence of dependents might be expected to decrease mobility. Children and elderly dependents are less able to travel around the city and, hence, more neighborhood oriented than the nonelderly adults in the family. The ties they form would tend to increase the intangible cost of moving. This is especially true of children in school. Parents might tend to value continuity in the education of their children.

---

[f]In terms of the model, the S function for larger or better housing increases in relative value with increased income.

[g]The median length of time between marriage and birth of the last child has been estimated at 10 years; the median time to marriage of the last child at 31 years. See Paul C. Glick and Robert Parke, Jr., "New Approaches In Studying the Life Cycle of the Family," *Demography*, 2:187-202 (1965). The figure of 20 was taken as marking an approximate divide between the period in which family increase is feasible and the period of decrease.

[h]To some extent the number of rooms is influenced by income. The demand for rooms, however, does not appear to be highly income elastic. See Louis Winnick, *American Housing and its Use: The Demand for Shelter Space* (New York: John Wiley and Sons, Inc., 1957), Chapter 3. The ratio of persons per room was found, moreover, to have the effect hypothesized above. See Chapters 5 and 6 of this book.

The growing of infants into toddlers, on the other hand, may lead to desire for increased space to accommodate children's play. That would lead to increased moving. Also, as children grow towards school age, parents may tend to move to place themselves in a neighborhood or municipality which is reported to have good schools. In summary, the presence of school age or elderly dependents is expected to decrease mobility, but dependents aged five or under may increase it.

Marriage can terminate by either death, divorce, or separation. Chevan's findings are that loss of a spouse through death does not lead directly to high mobility by the survivor. There is no apparent reason to contest that. Divorce or separation, however, must lead to moving by at least one spouse.

Income and race are frequently discussed in relation to residential mobility. It is not apparent, however, why income should have a direct effect on moving rates.[i] The effect of race and discrimination is also hard to hypothesize. That is, race could have conflicting effects. The housing choices open to blacks are restricted, and that lowers the quality of housing blacks occupy. Satisfaction with current housing may be assumed, therefore, to be lower than for whites and to lead to more moving. On the other hand, alternatives to currently occupied housing are also limited and, therefore, offer less incentive to move. That may cancel out the effect of higher levels of dissatisfaction.

A job move by the head of a household will alter his daily commuting pattern. That will alter the balance between residential land area consumed, the cost of that space and commuting costs (the last construed broadly).[3] A small change in job location will have, generally, a trivial effect. A larger change might lead to a situation where, by moving, the family can significantly improve its overall well-being. Even a small change, if it upsets transportation arrangements, might be important. For example, a person may change from a job within walking distance from a transit line running near the current home to one which is just beyond walking distance. Any job move, therefore, is expected to increase residential mobility. A longer job move should have a greater effect.

It is also possible that there will be considerable lag between a lengthening of the daily commute and a residential move to shorten the commute. Additional incentive may be needed, or a family may wait for a time which is propitious for individual reasons before moving. The probability of moving is expected to be higher, however, for families in which the head has a long commute.

Retiring or starting work after some nonemployed status may have a twofold effect. Commuting is entirely eliminated or introduced as a consideration for residential location; and income changes sharply, thus altering consumption possibilities. Both effects should lead to higher residential mobility.

Neighborhoods have certain social status, or class, connotations. People who feel that the class ranking of their neighborhood is lower than their own rank, or the rank they would like to attain, are hypothesized to be more prone to move

---

[i]It may have an indirect effect through tenure.

than those who feel on a par with their surroundings and neighbors. Assuming a family chose an appropriate neighborhood when they last moved, any upward change in the social status ranking of the head's job should decrease satisfaction with the neighborhood and increase the probability of a move. The income change which is likely to accompany the status change would reinforce the tendency. On the downward side, an income change is also likely. While, in that event, a move may not be desired, the income reduction may reduce effective demand for space and other amenities, thus leading to a move.

The Tenure Decision

The tenure decision, like the moving decision, is hypothesized to be influenced by the interaction of several factors. The list includes the length of time a family expects to remain at the next address, the cost of moving for each tenure, the family's tastes and desires, its income and assets, race, and the offerings of the sales and rental sectors of the housing market. Most of these can be construed as acting through their effect on the cost of housing over the anticipated period of residence in the new home, with the cost defined to include the discounted cost of the next move.

On an annual basis, owning a home costs less than renting the same dwelling. A full comparison of the economy of ownership and rental, however, must take into account the cost of selling. Shelton[4] estimates all fees in a sale as 7 percent of the value of the house. He estimates the annual net saving from owning to be 2.0 percent of the value of the house for a family in the 33 percent income tax bracket. Shelton overlooks, however, the effect of deducting mortgage interest and local property taxes from income subject to federal income taxes.[j] With these taken into account, and Shelton's other assumptions kept intact, savings for a family in the 33 percent tax bracket appear to be 3.5 percent of house value. For a family in the 20 percent tax bracket, which is more nearly typical of middle income (say $4,000 to $8,000 taxable income), annual savings are approximately 2.5 percent of value.[k]

With annual savings of 2.5 to 3.5 percent of house value, a family must remain in a house two to three years (ignoring time discount) before ownership becomes financially worthwhile. Over a shorter period, the cost of selling outweighs the expected savings from ownership. Furthermore, arranging the purchase, mortgage, and so on, is more onerous than renting. That adds a

[j]Shelton at one point dismisses the income tax advantage to homeowners on the ground that landlords also deduct the items mentioned. The landlord, however, is only acting as a pass-through. The occupant ultimately pays the expenses, whether he is renting or a homeowner. But only the homeowner can deduct them from his taxable income.

[k]The interest rates assumed by Shelton, and for the estimates above, are below the current levels, but are close to rates prevailing around 1960. Shelton assumed six percent mortgage interest and eight percent return on equity.

nonmonetary cost which would deter purchase unless substantial net gains (synonymous with long residence) are anticipated.

The type of housing desired also affects tenure choice. Within 10 years of marriage, the median family has its last child. (See note 8.) That event generally coincides with maximum family size and, presumably, maximum space preference. Both indoor and outdoor space is desired. A single family house is indicated, and such housing is generally offered for sale rather than rent.

Both supply and demand considerations account for the preponderance of ownership of such housing. Shelton has estimated the management cost of rental property at five percent of gross rent. It would probably be higher for single-family housing, since the scale economies of apartment house management would be missing. That would broaden the ownership-rental cost gap. (It might be lower for tenement housing with a resident owner. The resident owner neither has to hire an agent nor travel to his property for management chores.)

On the demand side, couples that have been married several years generally have become less mobile, regardless of tenure. They might reasonably anticipate remaining at one residence for several years after a move, thus making the net economies of ownership positive. In other words, the cost spread between owning and renting is greater for single-family housing, and the family which has grown to a size to desire such housing is also likely to be stable enough to realize ownership advantages. As a result, relatively few families might be expected to desire to rent single family houses.

That leaves the question of why small units are not offered for sale. Part of the reason may be that, given the greater mobility of the young, most of the demand[1] for small units is from small, new, families which can anticipate continued high mobility. For those families, purchase would not be desirable, and demand for small purchasable units would, therefore, be small. On the supply side, smaller units tend to be supplied in multifamily structures, so as to achieve high densities in terms of units per acre. Sale of such units would involve the complexities of cooperative or condominium arrangements. At least one of the usual cost disadvantages of rental housing, management expenses, would be kept. In any event, cooperatives and condominiums were not an important part of the housing supply in 1960 in the area under study.[m]

To summarize this point, young, small families are relatively unlikely to purchase when moving. Larger family size and increased number of years married will increase the probability of purchase. Space demands, the costs of the nature of the housing supply, and the effect of reduced mobility on the cost comparison between owning and renting have this effect.

---

[1]Demand is construed in the marginal, or active, sense, not cross-sectional. (See Chapter 2, for further discussion of this distinction.)

[m]In South Florida cooperates and condominiums are common. There is a high inmigration of elderly couples and unattached individuals who intend to make that area their permanent retirement residence. While such households would tend to want small units, they are in a position to enjoy the financial benefits of ownership. They create a demand for apartments which can be bought.

The effect of years married, however, is not linear. After peak family size is passed, the desire for space may be expected to diminish. Diminished family size and space demand, coupled with the nature of the housing supply, can be expected to militate, in the event of a move, for rental. They counteract the effect of the reduced mobility of older families.

Another factor affecting residential mobility expectations, and hence, tenure decision, is expected job stability. A family head who anticipates changing jobs, or whose job security is uncertain, would be less likely to purchase than one who expects to stay at his current job.

While owner occupancy is cheaper than renting the same dwelling, housing units available for sale tend to be larger and newer than rental units. Single-family house neighborhoods are also considered more desirable socially than multi-family or mixed areas. That, too, would make it difficult to find purchase units which are available cheaply. Low income families are less likely, therefore, to buy than middle- and upper-income families. In addition, the graduated income tax makes the savings from ownership proportionally higher for high income families than for low and, thereby, reinforces the income effect. (That was illustrated above.)

The income effect is further reinforced by the capital requirements for purchase. Low income families are less likely than others to have the liquid resources needed for down payment and settlement costs.

The income hypothesis applies not only to total family income but also to income per capita. A large family tends to spend less on housing than a small family of the same income.[5] Typically it has higher nonhousing demands on its budget, which reduce its effective demand for housing.

Prior tenure may be significantly related to tenure choice in two ways. Ownership typically involves more chores and responsibilities than renting, and a house, as opposed to an apartment—a choice usually implied by the tenure choice—suggests a different life style. To some extent, therefore, tenure choice will reflect the family's subjective evaluation of the nonmonetary burdens of ownership and its preferences regarding type of dwelling. Prior tenure gives some indication of the nature of such evaluations by the family.

The second significance of prior tenure is that those who owned generally will have realized some cash equity from the sale of their former home. That can furnish the down payment and settlement costs for a new one. Furthermore, in the inflationary housing market that has prevailed for many years, an owner is likely to have a financial gain from the sale of his home. To avoid capital gains tax on the profit, he must purchase another house which is at least equal in value to the one he sold.

Race and Tenure

Nonwhites have traditionally found their choice of housing more limited than that of whites. Typically, they are restricted to the older sections of cities where multifamily structures are predominant. While some blacks are able to buy homes in new single-family neighborhoods, they must exert considerable effort. Blacks who buy homes in predominantly white neighborhoods at some distance from established black areas get little help from real estate brokers.[6] They also face some severe social risks.[7] In the City of Philadelphia, the tendency of black neighborhoods to expand predominantly at their fringe has been documented.[8] Blacks who worked in outlying areas did not have the option, by and large, of following their jobs to the suburbs where most of the new single-family homes were being built.

Another aspect of being confined to central areas is that blacks, whether or not they desire centrality, must pay the high location rent of central neighborhoods. In addition, there is evidence that they pay more than whites for comparable housing in comparable locations. Rapkin and Grigsby found evidence of a small premium paid by blacks in Philadelphia.[n] Ridker, in a study of the St. Louis metropolitan area, found higher values for single-family houses in census tracts with higher percentages of nonwhites, even when centrality and several other conditions which might affect price were controlled for.[9]

Black renters also face discrimination. Such discrimination and the price-quality effects have been described often.[10] Whether the price effect of discrimination was greater for rental or purchase of housing in the Penn Jersey area in the few years up to 1960 is unknown.

The geographic nature of discrimination leads to the expectation of less opportunity for blacks, relative to whites, to buy than rent. The location of the ghettos, and the paucity of new sales housing open to blacks,[11] would lead to a relatively low ratio of sales to rental offerings to blacks. As a consequence, black movers might be expected to be less likely than comparable whites to purchase a home. The supply simply is not there.[12] Any surge of black demand for home purchase would have required a large increase in the prices paid by black buyers—given the existing racial restrictions—thereby shifting the cost comparison between ownership and rental for blacks markedly in favor of renting. The change itself would have acted to restrain the purchase demand.

The Unmarried

Unmarried heads of households are a highly heterogeneous group. Included are single, divorced, separated, and widowed people of both sexes, with and without dependents. They do have some things, however, in common. By and large, as mentioned earlier, there is only one adult who has decision-making responsibility for the household. Exceptions are unrelated roommates and people living with

---

[n]The difference showed in direct comparison of purchase prices, and in that the housing prices in blocks which blacks were entering were noticeably higher than would have been expected in the absence of active black demand. See Rapkin and Grigsby, p. 63 and pp. 90-105.

either elderly dependents or grown children. Households consisting of room-mates can readily break up. The grown children living with a parent who is the head of the household would not be expected to have the same weight vote as his parent, and the same might be true of elderly dependents. It would be easier, therefore, for an unmarried household head who is dissatisfied for any reason with his housing to decide to move. There is less restraint within the household and there are fewer persons to be satisfied in choosing another dwelling. For that reason, the unmarried might be expected to respond more readily than married couples to such stimuli as job changes.

Another common feature of the unmarried is that most of them can get married or remarried. (The separated cannot.) That event is quite likely to lead to a move. The probability of marriage may be expected to decline with age (see below).

The effect on mobility of the factors discussed in connection with married people should be similar in direction with the unmarried, although differing in degree. Owners can be expected to move less than renters. Mobility is expected to decline with age. Larger family size is hypothesized to lower mobility, but the children under school age are expected to increase it. Increases[o] and decreases in family size would increase probability of a move, as would job change. Change in the social status of a job might be expected to have less influence, however, than with married couples. There is less likely to be the desire to secure what is considered a fitting neighborhood for family life—since there is less likely to be a family. As with married couples, there is no reason to expect income to influence mobility, and the effect of race is too uncertain to be hypothesized.

Choice of Tenure by the Unmarried

As with moving, many of the expectations concerning choice of tenure when moving are qualitatively similar for unmarried and married. The tendency to buy would tend to increase with age, income, and family size and to be lower for blacks. Prior ownership would lead to increased propensity to buy.

There are, however, some major differences. The symbolic value of an owned home for family life would tend to be lower. That may cause the propensity to purchase to be low in general.

A more concrete consideration is the expectation of marriage (or remarriage) and, hence, future mobility. If expectations are realistic, the anticipation of first marriage for women should fall to a very low level by age 35 or 40. For widows or divorcees, expectation of remarriage should become rather low during the

---

[o]Increases, other than those resulting from marrying during the period of observation, would be rare.

40s.[P] For men, the appropriate ages might be a little older than for women. For younger unmarried heads, who may have reasonable expectation of marriage, we might expect a low propensity to buy a home. Such a purchase may, in fact, seem to many to be an act of resignation.

[P]Data on this subject is sketchy. In England and Wales, in 1951, the percentage of widows remarrying annually was four percent for those aged 40 to 49 and one percent for those 50 to 59. The percent of spinsters marrying was four percent for those aged 35 to 39, 2 percent for those 40 to 49, and one-half percent if in their 50s. See Peter Marris, *Widows and Their Families* (London: Routledge and Kegan Paul, 1958), p. 60.

Appendix 3A: Housing Market Conditions

The assertion that each move involves a tenure choice requires the assumption that housing units in which a family could accommodate itself are available in each tenure category. Vacancy rates in the study area tend to support the assumption. In 1960, vacancy rates were moderate and somewhat higher than in 1950. For the Philadelphia and Trenton SMSA's combined, they were as follows:[13]

	1950	1960
Total	1.2%	2.8%
Ownership Supply	0.9%	1.3%
Rental Supply	1.8%	5.9%

Another implicit assumption of the model is that housing supply conditions did not change significantly during the period of investigation. The model, as developed below, refers almost exclusively to factors affecting demand by individual households.

The movements of the rental housing component of the B.L.S. Consumer Price Index for Philadelphia tend to support this assumption. Rents rose in the Philadelphia area in the decade, 1950-1960, but less than in the United States as a whole. The rise was considerably less than in the Boston area, and practically identical with the Washington, D.C., area (See Table 3A-1). That is, rent levels indicate that no particular stringency or glut of housing occurred in the study area during that period.

Interest rates, which are of crucial importance to home buyers, were also reasonably stable during the period under investigation. Between September, 1957, and June, 1965—a period which more than covers the study period—returns on conventional mortgages fluctuated nationally within a range of 0.76 percent, and returns on FHA-insured mortgages, 0.86 percent.[14] Returns during 1960 on the two types were 6.22 and 6.18 percent, respectively.[15]

Table 3A-1
Price Index for Residential Rents, Urbanized Areas (1957-59 = 100.)

	1950	1960
Philadelphia	83.6	103.3
Boston	75.1	108.4
Washington, D.C.	84.3	103.9
United States	79.1	103.1

Source: U.S. Bureau of the Census, *Statistical Abstract of the United States: 1968* (89th Edition), Tables 505 and 511.

During the late 1950s there was a trend towards lower down payment requirements and longer period for mortgage repayment. It is illustrated in Table 3A-2, which shows the average down payment and maturity terms for first mortgages in 1955 and 1959. Those changes facilitated home purchase and increased somewhat the propensity of movers to buy. The changes appear, however, to have been gradual enough to permit the achievement of significant results by means of the approach employed here.

Table 3A-2

Average Down Payment and Maturity for First Mortgages, 1955 and 1959

	Mortgage Type		
	FHA	VA	S&L Conventional
Down Payment (%)			
1955 new	15.1	5.3	37.1
1955 existing	19.0	11.6	
1959 new	7.7	3.3	33.4
1959 existing	10.4	11.0	
Maturity (years)			
1955 new	25.6	27.4	not available
1955 existing	22.7	22.2	
1959 new	28.8	28.8	not available
1959 existing	25.2	23.5	

Source: *Federal Reserve Bulletin*, 46:843 (1960).

4

Method of Investigation: A Problem in Marginal and Contingent Probability

The Probability Model

The decision to move and the decision to buy or to rent housing are being viewed as closely related but conceptually separable problems. This leads, as stated earlier, to examining mobility and the decision by movers to buy or rent as a problem in marginal and contingent probability. That is, home purchase is viewed as a decision to be made after, and contingent on, a decision to move. The decision to move, on the other hand, is treated as independent of the tenure choice decision.

The latter is admittedly oversimplified. The net appeal of dwellings alternative to the current one is in part a function of the tenure status of the alternatives. (Refer to Equations (3.2) through (3.4), inclusive, and inequality (3.5) in Chapter 3.) Nevertheless, the working assumption that the moving decision is independent leads to intelligible and worthwhile results. By way of contrast, examination of the overall, or marginal, probability of home purchase has been seen to be simply unproductive; the conditional-probability approach is more rewarding.[a]

The investigation is carried out by means of linear probability models. The models resemble linear regression models. Parameters in fact are estimated by exactly the same algorithm (least squares) and computer programs. Operationally, the main difference is that binary dummy variables—here representing moving over the two-year period of observation or tenure choice—are the dependent variables. In regression, the dependent variables typically are continuous.

In the moving problem, the dependent variable is set at zero in cases of no move and at 1.0 for cases of one or more moves. In the tenure choice problem, a value of 1.0 represents home purchase. Independent variables in the moving problem represent family composition at the beginning of the period, housing arrangements, age of head, life cycle events, job changes, distance of such changes, distance from work at the beginning of the period, and family income. A similar but shorter list of variables was used in the tenure choice problem.

The designated values of the dependent variables are the actual, known, probabilities of moving in a two-year period or of purchasing a home, given a

---

[a]Symbolically, if moving is represented by X_1 and home purchase by X_2, it is assumed that $P(X_1, X_2) = P(X_1) \cdot P(X_2|X_1)$, and that $P(X_1)$ is independent of X_2. $P(X_1)$ and $P(X_2|X_1)$ are then examined individually.

move. The estimated values of y, therefore, may be taken as estimates of these probabilities, and the regression coefficients as estimates of the influence of each independent variable upon the probabilities. This method was used by Orcutt, et al.,[1] Lee,[2] and Maisel,[3] and it is described by Johnston[4] and by Warner.[5]

Relationship to Discriminant Analysis

Genealogically the method employed here is closer perhaps to discriminant analysis than to multiple regression. Discriminant analysis applies to problems of determining in which of two or more distinct natural groups an unassigned observation or event falls. The groups in question here are movers and nonmovers in the one problem, and purchasers and renters in the other. The observations in the two problems are households and moving households, respectively.

Assume a sample of n observations of, say, m independent variables. The discriminant problem is to develop a function of these independent variables that allows assigning a new observation, for which group identity is unknown, to one of the groups. The discriminant function is, of course, estimated from a sample for which group identities are known.

Taking the two-group problem, the observations in the two groups can be assumed to have different mean values of the independent variables. The objective of linear discriminant analysis is to find the linear function of the X_i's,

$$D = \sum_{i=1}^{m} d_i X_i,$$

that best differentiates between members of the two groups. The criterion of best is that the probability of misclassification be minimized. The resultant operational rule for calculating the normal, or estimating, equations for the d_i's, is that the ratio of the within-group variance of D to the difference between group means of D be minimized. (It is conventionally assumed that the within-group variances of the X_i's and of D are the same for both groups.[6]) These estimating equations are used to estimate the d_i's from data in a sample for which group identities are known. D can then be calculated and used to assign any new observation to the more probable group. The new observation is classified with the group whose group mean D value is closer to the D value for that observation. (A more mathematical discussion of discriminant analysis is contained in Appendix 4A.)

There is a direct correspondence between two-group linear discriminant analysis and the linear probability functions employed here. Let the two groups from a sample of size n be considered as two subsamples of size n_1 and n_2, respectively, with $n_1 + n_2 = n$. Assign a value of n_2/n to the dependent variable

y_1 for members of the first group, and $-n_1/n$ to y_2, the dependent variable for the second group. Then $\bar{y} = 0$. A regression of y on the X_i's, where the latter are transformed into deviations about their means, will yield an equation,

$$\hat{y} = \sum_{i=1}^{m} b_i X_i.$$

where $\hat{y}$ is the discriminant value. Fisher has shown that the b_i's differ only by a constant multiplier from the d_i's of an orthodox discriminant analysis. That is, $b_i = K \cdot d_i$, where K is a constant.[7] The linear probability model has the same equivalence as Fisher's linear regression, differing only in that it also has an intercept term.[b]

Empirical Analysis Procedures, and Some Caveats

In the equations discussed in the following chapters, most of the independent variables resemble the dependent in that they are binary in form. A value of 1.0 represents a certain status (e.g., retired at the start of the period of observation) or event (retirement), and a value of 0.0 the absence of the status or event. Sets of related variables exhaust all but one possibility for classifying a family or head of household. For example, retired and other nonemployed heads are indicated by two binary variables. "Employed" in this case exhausts the possibilities, but it is not explicitly represented.

Variables representing events also imply a categorization of the observations. For example, the birth of one or more children in the period of observation is indicated by a binary variable. The unspecified group consists of families which did not experience a birth.

The choice of the unspecified group is essentially arbitrary. Where one group may be considered by tradition to be typical, it was chosen. An example is a family of four or more consisting of a married couple and their children. Where no such group can be chosen, the group expected a priori to be the largest, or one of the larger, was chosen. In the case of events, the nonoccurrence of the event was considered typical.

---

[b]The y values assigned here differ from Fisher's only by $\bar{y}$. Take $y_1 = 1.0$ and $y_2 = 0.0$. Then,

(1) $\bar{y} = n_1/n$
(2) $y_1 - \bar{y} = n/n - n_1/n = n_2/n$
(3) $y_2 - \bar{y} = -n_1/n$

The terms on the right of (2) and (3) are the same as those assigned by Fisher. The X values are also the same except for subtraction of mean values. In short, only a shift of the origin to the point of means would be required to make linear probability functions identical to Fisher's regression about the means. The slope, or b_i values, would be unaffected.

To illustrate the interpretation of the coefficients of binary variables, assume that three family-size categories are differentiated; S_1 and S_2 are represented by dummy variables and S_3 is unspecified. Assume that birth of a child is also specified. If there are no interaction effects between birth of a child and family size categories—that is, the effect of variables is strictly additive—coefficients of S_1 and S_2 would represent simply the difference in mobility between their categories and S_3. It seems much more likely, however, that there are some unspecified interaction effects. These may be statistically and heuristically insignificant, thereby justifying not representing them. They will, however, have an effect on the estimated coefficients. Specifying S_1 and S_2 is not exactly equivalent to specifying S_2 and S_3. Similarly, in dichotomous cases, the coefficient of X_i (a dummy variable) is not the exact negative of the coefficient that would have been estimated for not -X_i. This qualification should be borne in mind when reading Chapters 5, 6, and 7.

In the initial experiments with the data, all scalar quantities, such as age and income, were represented both linearly and by their square.[c] The purpose of the quadratic formulation was to test for nonlinear effects. The double representation (linear and squared) was retained only where preliminary results justified it.

Additivity of the effects of the independent variables was generally assumed. By and large that was required by the large number of factors being considered. Comprehensive specifications of interaction between variables was not feasible.

The two major exceptions to the additivity assumption are the variables used for partitioning the samples, tenure and marital status. To partition the samples and calculate the regressions separately for each part entails, in effect, investigating the interaction of the variables used for partitioning with all the others.

Some additional interaction between factors is specified in the variable lists. For example, the variable representing "2 [people] in 1-2 [rooms], or 3 or more in 3 rooms" is a limited representation of the interaction of family size and number of rooms in the dwelling. Also, the family composition variables represent limited cross-tabulation by characteristics which could have been represented only by marginal classification (i.e., one-way tabulation).

The linear probability model being used does involve certain problems. The estimated probability of moving is not constrained to the 0.0–1.0 range. Furthermore, the binary nature of the dependent variable leads to heteroskedasticity in the disturbance term. The first problem is not serious here. It is recognized that point estimates of a parameter can err on either side of a true value. An estimate which happens to be impossible in any realistic sense might be as close to the true value as an estimate which errs by an equal amount in the opposite direction. For example, 1.01 might be considered as good an estimate of a true value of 0.99 as is 0.97.[d]

---

[c]In some instances, the quantities were divided by a constant so as to reduce the absolute variance of the variables involved. That was desirable in the case of variables with large variance in order to maintain the accuracy of the regression calculations.

[d]A value of 1.01 might pose a problem in an applied study; for example, a housing market study which includes a forecast of moving as part of the demand estimate.

Heteroskedasticity, however, remains. The effect is to reduce the efficiency of the estimating procedure, as compared to the efficiency achieved under the usual linear regression assumptions. That problem, however, has not been overwhelming. Meaningful results have been obtained. The large size of the sample is an important saving factor.

In developing the statistical models, several more variables were considered than were retained in the equations. The models as presented contain the maximum number of variables that can enter with a t value of 1.0 or greater. To have included more variables in the models would have increased the standard error of estimate. Furthermore, in earlier experiments with the data, estimated regression coefficients for variables with t values under 1.0 frequently had the wrong sign in comparison with reasonable expectations. That is, a t value of 1.0 appears in practice to mark a division between estimates of regression coefficients that on heuristic grounds are credible and those that are problematic.

In addition, where two variables were closely correlated, and that correlation led to results judged spurious on nonstatistical grounds, one of the variables was excluded from the equation. That led on occasion to a reduction in the t value of the other variable which was involved to below 1.0, and hence the exclusion of both variables from the model.

Finally, the calculations were performed by means of a step-wise multiple-regression computer program. Calculations were not simply terminated, however, when all remaining variables showed t under 1.0. Rather, the program was allowed to calculate the full equations. The full equations were checked to be sure that the findings were not distorted by the order in which variables were "stepped" into the regression calculations. The step-in feature of the program, that is, was used as a convenience. It was not the final arbiter for the inclusion or exclusion of any variables.

Data

The investigation makes use of the Supplemental Home Interview (SHI) conducted in 1960 by the Penn Jersey Transportation Study. The SHI sample consisted of a subsample of the home interview survey conducted for conventional traffic planning purposes.[8]

The SHI contains up to twelve years of family and work history for the head of each household interviewed.[e] (If a head of household was less than 30 years old at the time of the interview, the survey history went back only until his eighteenth birthday.) The data recorded included job history, residential history, and household information. (See Appendix 4B for further discussion of the SHI.)

---

[e]It must be emphasized that the histories recorded in the SHI focused upon the head of the household, not his family as it existed at the time of interview. One consequence is that family and residential histories of wives prior to the wives' current marriage were not recorded. Also, there are no work histories for wives. For families headed by widows, the late husband's work history was not recorded.

The information contained in the SHI requires further processing before analysis can be carried out. For purposes of examining moving, moves and events which may be considered to affect propensity to move were observed for each family for the two-year period preceding the interview. In addition, variables were extracted to describe the head of household, the family, and the family's housing supply at the beginning of the two-year observation period.

The SHI contains complete information on 5,808 households. Not all of the data, however, was used in this study. Household heads for which less than two years' history is available were excluded. In effect, that means that no household headed by a person less than 20 years old at the time of interview is included. Those who migrated into the region during the two years preceding the interview were also excluded. Migration is a separate problem. As it is, the region covers nine counties.[f] It is likely, therefore, that some relatively large residential moves, which conventionally would be counted as migration, are included in this study as local movement. An alternative is to follow conventional practice, designating all intercounty moves as migration. That would lead to excluding many city-to-suburb, suburb-to-suburb, and suburb-to-city moves. Such moves do not involve the kind of change in community affiliation that may be considered the definitional characteristic of migration, and they are an important part of overall residential movement within the urban area. It would not have been acceptable, therefore, to exclude them.

Households formed in the two years preceding the interview were also excluded.[g] Household formation is important in relation to housing demand, but it is a different phenomenon from moving. Including it in the present investigation would obscure the analysis.

After the exclusions, 5,198 cases remained. Of those, 1,230 had unmarried heads, and 3,968 married;[h] 702 of the unmarried householders, and 3,085 of the married, were owners. Analysis of moving performance by the four groups (married and unmarried, owners and renters) was carried out separately.

In the tenure choice problem, the units of observation were intraarea moves. Inmigration and housing choice by new households were excluded. The sample

---

[f]Nine counties participated in the Penn Jersey Transportation Study. All interviewing was conducted within those nine counties. For analytic purposes, however, two additional counties were considered part of the urban area: New Castle County, Delaware, and Salem County, New Jersey. Interviewees who were living in one of those two counties two years earlier were also considered local movers. This involved only a small number of households.

[g]That exclusion encompasses households whose head was in an institutional residence two years earlier.

[h]It might be considered worthwhile to divide the unmarried further according to marital status; for example, widowed, other previously married, and single might be considered as relevant groups. These groups tend to differ widely in age, prior experience, and, presumably, in current needs and expectations. There is a tradeoff, however, between the number of subdivisions of the sample and the number of variables whose influence on moving can be examined. The compromise made has been to separate the married from the unmarried but to leave all the unmarried together.

of moves was partitioned into those by married heads of household (608 moves), and those by unmarried (264 moves). Tenure choice was analyzed separately for the two groups.

Appendix 4A: More on Discriminant Analysis

The Problem

Assume a sample of n observations, of which n_1 fall into group 1, and n_2 into group 2. For each member of the sample, m independent variables, X_i, have been observed. (These variables may be thought to represent characteristics of the population.) The problem is to find a function of the X_i's that can be used to classify any new observation reliably into one of the two groups.

Distance as a Basis for Discrimination

The following is a simple but relatively inefficient method of classification.

To equalize the influences of each variable, transform the X_i into standardized variables, Z_i (i.e., Z_i represents standard deviations from the mean of X_i). For each of the two groups of observations, group means, $_1\overline{Z}_i$ and $_2\overline{Z}_i$, exist, such that

$$n_1 \cdot {}_1\overline{Z}_i + n_2 \cdot {}_2\overline{Z}_i = 0. \tag{4A.1}$$

An observation from one group can be expected to have a set of attributes, or profile, represented in transformed variables as $Z_1, Z_2, \ldots Z_m$, that more closely resembles the means for that group than the means for the other group.

To determine closeness, define distance between the individual and group average profiles as the square root of the sum of squares of the differences between individual values, Z_i, and group means, $_g\overline{Z}_i$. The distance squared is:

$$_gS^2 = \sum_{i=1}^{m} (Z_i - {}_g\overline{Z}_i)^2. \tag{4A.2}$$

For an observation in group 1, it is to be expected that $_1S^2 < {}_2S^2$. This can be taken as a rule of classification.

Discriminant Analysis

The multivariate distributions of the two groups about their mean profiles, however, can be expected to overlap in such a way as to cause some erroneous classifications from the rule stated above. The objective of discriminant analysis is to develop, if possible, a more efficient function; that is, one whose distribution is such as to give lower—or the minimum—probability of misclassification. (Misclassification cannot be totally eliminated.)

43

The minimization can be achieved by deriving a function, the ratio of whose within-groups variance to between-groups variance is a minimum. Equal within-group variance and covariance of the X_i's for the two groups are usually assumed. The distribution of the observations within each group is also assumed to be multivariate normal.

The algebraic problem becomes that of estimating the set of d_i's in the function,

$$D = \sum_{i=1}^{m} d_i X_i, \tag{4A.3}$$

such that the ratio of total, or pooled, within-groups variance to between-groups variance of D is minimized. That is the problem as stated in Chapter 4.

Let G represent an $(n \times m)$ matrix of the observations, X, transformed into absolute deviations about the means; $_1\overline{G}$ and $_2\overline{G}$ two $(m \times 1)$ vectors of within-group means of the X_i's; and d an $(m \times 1)$ vector of the d_i's; also, let,

$$r = {}_1\overline{G} - {}_2\overline{G}. \tag{4A.4}$$

Then, under the rather strong assumptions given above about the distribution of X, and hence of G, the solution of the estimating equation for d is,[9]

$$d \propto (G'G)^{-1} r. \tag{4A.5}$$

Note that the solution is determinate only up to an arbitrary constant. That is, if the vector, d, is a solution, $c \cdot d$ is also, where c is any constant.

Now, b, a vector of the coefficients of a least squares linear regression, is estimated as,

$$b = (G'G)^{-1} G'h, \tag{4A.6}$$

where h is an $(n \times 1)$ vector of the independent variable, y, transformed into absolute deviations about the mean, $\overline{y}$.

If y was originally set—as in the linear probability model—at 1.0 for group 1 and 0. for group 2, then it can be shown that,[i]

[i]From note b in Chapter 4,

    i) $\overline{y} = n_1 / n$.

    ii) $y_1 - \overline{y} = n_2 / n$.

    iii) $y_2 - \overline{y} = -n_1 / n$.

Then, in matrix terms,

    iv) $G'h = \dfrac{n_2}{n} n_1 \cdot {}_1\overline{G} - \dfrac{n_1}{n} n_2 \cdot {}_2\overline{G}$.

    v) $= \dfrac{n_1 n_2}{n} ({}_1\overline{G} - {}_2\overline{G})$

$$G'h = \frac{n_1 n_2}{n} \cdot (_1\overline{G} - _2\overline{G}) \qquad (4A.7)$$

$$= \frac{n_1 n_2}{n} \cdot r \qquad (4A.8)$$

Substituting (4A.8) into (4A.6),

$$b = \frac{n_1 n_2}{n} \cdot (G'G)^{-1}r \qquad (4A.9)$$

and, therefore,

$$b \propto d. \qquad (4A.10)$$

That is, the coefficients of discriminant analysis, and of a linear probability model which employs the ordinary least squares regression algorithm, are proportional. Since the discriminant analysis solution is determined only up to an arbitrary constant, the difference between the two solution values recedes into triviality. The assumptions concerning the distribution of X, however, are different for the two models.[10]

Typically in discriminant analysis, the critical value for classifying observations is $(\overline{D}_1 + \overline{D}_2)/2$, where $\overline{D}_1$ and $\overline{D}_2$ represent means of D for groups 1 and 2, respectively. The corresponding critical value in linear probability analysis is $(\overline{y}_1 + \overline{y}_2)/2$, where the values in parentheses are group means of the estimated probability of being in group 1. There is nothing sacrosanct, however, about these values, If the cost of misclassification in one direction is greater than the opposite error, the decision value can be adjusted accordingly.

Appendix 4B: The Supplemental Home Interview

Sample

The sample for the SHI was drawn from the regular home interview sample of the Penn Jersey Transportation Study. The home interview had a sampling rate of 4 percent in the more densely built-up parts of the urban area. In the outer part of the survey area, a rate of 10 percent was used. Before drawing the sample for the SHI for the outer part of the survey area, an intermediate sample of 40 percent of the home interview sample was drawn. Then, taking that subsample and the entire home interview sample for the inner part, a final selection was made of families to be interviewed in the SHI. For this final step, the sampling rate was 10 percent for families with less than $25,000 income, 50 percent for families with $25,000 income or more, and 20 percent for families in which income was unknown or where the original home interview attempt was unsuccessful.[11]

Response rates varied among the sampling strata. The range was 91.0 to 97.7 percent. The unadjusted sampling ratio varied from 1:50 to 1:250. Adjusted for noninterview in the SHI, the ratios ran from 1:54 to 1:264. Excluding those with income over $25,000, 154 out of 6,176 attempted interviews, the range of the adjusted ratios was 1:134 to 1:264. In general, those registering previous noninterview, or failing to report income in the home interview, were represented almost twice as heavily in the complete interviews as those who gave income information in the first instance (excluding those fortunate few with incomes over $25,000). One might speculate on the effects on quality of weighting a sample in favor of reluctant respondents. On the other hand, the high response rates from all strata are reassuring. (See Table 4B-1.)

Data

The Supplemental Home Interview recorded the history of the person who was the head of the household at the time of the interview. It must be recognized, of course, that that person may not have been the head of a household throughout the period covered. He may, for example, have gone from being a grown child in his parents' home to an institutional setting such as army or college; and from there to having his own household.

The household information includes marital status changes for the head. For each person who lived with the head it includes the date of entrance to and "exit" from the household in which the head was living, and the relationship to head of household. The "exit" of a family member may in fact be the exit of the

47

Table 4B-1

Interviews and Responses by Interview Stratum and Income—Number of Households

Stratum and Income	Interviews Attempted	Interviews Completed	Percent Complete	Representation Ratio	
				Intended	Actual
Total	6,176	5,844[a]	94.6	–	–
H.I. noninterview	1,249	1,137	91.0	125	137
Income not reported in H.I.	1,221	1,138	93.2	125	134
Income to $2,000	263	257	97.7	250	256
$2,000 to 3,999	715	677	94.7	250	264
$4,000 to 6,499	1,366	1,311	96.0	250	260
$6,500 to 9,999	904	882	97.6	250	256
$10,000 to 24,999	304	299	98.4	250	254
$25,000 & above	154	143	92.9	50	54

[a]Includes 36 interviews with only partial information.

Source: Chevan, Albert: *Moving in a Metropolitan Area* (unpublished Ph.D. dissertation, University of Pennsylvania, 1968), Table 1, p. 19.

head from an earlier household in which he was a member. For those in the household at the time of interview, the interview date and designated exit date are the same.

The information on the head's residences includes location, dates of entrance and exit, tenure, number of rooms (if not a group residence), type of structure by number of dwelling units (or nondwelling-unit category), and physical structure type (e.g., detached, row). There is no data, however, on value, rent, or physical condition.

The job history includes job location, occupation, and an occupational status rating. The last is based, by and large, on the ratings developed by Warner et al.[12] The ratings were devised as part of a more general social status ranking scheme. All occupations are ranked on a scale of one to seven. The tabular presentation of the rating scheme also groups jobs within broad sectors (e.g., "white collar workers"). Within sectors, the ratings appear to be correlated with income. A change in the rating, therefore, may be taken as a proxy for income change. A change in the rating might also indicate a change in the individual's self-conception of his social class position. Lack of change in the rating, however, does not necessarily indicate income stability. Even within any sector and rating, considerable income variation is possible.

The SHI contains data only on current income (i.e., 1959). No attempt was made to record income in earlier years.

5 Moving by the Married: Empirical Analysis

Two Subgroups

Marital status and tenure—whether one owns or rents his home—were expected a priori to be two of the major influences upon residential moving behavior. For that reason, the observations from the SHI were divided into four groups on the basis of those variables at the beginning of the two-year period of observation, and the residential mobility of each group was examined separately. The results for two of those groups, married owners and married renters, are discussed in this chapter.

As anticipated, the two tenure groups contrast strongly in their moving behavior. Approximately 39 percent of the renters represented by the sample moved in the two-year period. In comparison, under 7 percent of the owners moved. (See Table 5-1.)

The difference in average age of the two groups may have contributed to the difference in moving. Owners were 49 on average, renters 43. On the other hand, even older renters move much more than owners taken as a whole. Renters 40 years old and over moved approximately four times as frequently as owners (Table 5-1, column 4); those under 40 moved eight times as frequently (Table 5-1, column 3).

The average age of owners was expected to be greater than that of renters. Many families start married life in rented quarters and then become owners. After that, they do not tend to go back to renting. The life cycle-tenure relationship is also reflected in other variables. Twenty percent of renters are couples married under 20 years, and 12 percent are families of three with a young child. Thus, 32 percent are small families in an early to early-to-middle phase of the family life cycle. Among owners, only 12 percent are small families in a comparable phase.

Twenty-four percent of renters are small families in the declining or stable phase—i.e., couples married 20 years or more, or couples with only one child, and that child five or over. Thirty-one percent of owners fall into one of these categories.

Owners were more likely than renters to have a relative other than their children in the home (13 percent compared to 8 percent). Nonrelatives were in the home of just under 1 percent of renters and just over 1 percent of owners.

A substantial majority of families in both categories, 65 percent of renters and 70 percent of owners, had one or more children in the family.

49

Table 5-1

Population Means[a] (Estimated) of Variables Used in Investigation, Married Household Heads

Var. No.	Variable	Renters (All)	Owners (All)	Renters Head Under 40	Renters Head 40 or More
–	Moved in two-year period	0.389	0.065	0.524	0.255
01	Age of head at interview	42.503	48.621	30.956	53.883
02	$Age^2 \div 100$	20.050	n.c.	9.789	30.153
03	Log_e (age of head)	3.697	3.851	3.421	3.968
04	2 persons, married 0-19 years at start[b]	0.199	0.080	0.217	0.183
05	2 persons, married 20 years or more[b]	0.127	0.163	0.000	0.253
06	3 persons, including child under 5[b]	0.116	0.039	0.223	0.011
07	3 persons, including child 5 or Over[b]	0.110	0.151	0.058	0.161
08	3 persons, including relative other than child[b]	0.016	0.029	0.007	0.026
09	4 persons or More, including Other relative[b]	0.060	0.102	0.054	0.066
10	Family size 7 or more[b]	0.076	0.051	0.075	0.076
11	Child(ren) present[b]	0.653	0.705	0.776	0.531
12	Other relative(s) in household[b]	0.076	0.131	0.061	0.092
13	Nonrelative(s) in household[b]	0.008	0.011	0.003	0.013
14	Spouse died in period	0.018	0.031	0.006	0.029
15	Separated or divorced in period	0.024	0.007	0.033	0.016
16	Dissolved and remarried in period	0.002	0.001	0.003	0.001
17	Child(ren) born in period	0.200	0.089	0.357	0.045
18	Other family size increase	0.017	0.025	0.014	0.019
19	Family size decrease, not dissolved	0.049	0.110	0.015	0.082
20	Head nonwhite or Puerto Rican	0.280	0.095	0.320	0.241
21	Family income ($1,000's)	5.926	7.631	5.300	6.543
22	Persons per room 0-0.25[b]	n.c.	0.036	n.c.	n.c.
23	Persons per room 0.26-0.50[b]	n.c.	0.426	n.c.	n.c.
24	Persons per room over 1.0[b]	0.175	0.043	0.229	0.121
25	2 in 1-2 rooms or 3 or more in 3 rooms[b]	0.109	0.006	0.139	0.080
26	3 or more persons in 1-2 rooms[b]	0.023	0.000	0.041	0.006
27	Owns multi-family structure[b]	n.c.	0.041	n.c.	n.c.
28	Hotel, motel or rooming house[b]	n.c.	0.002	n.c.	n.c.
29	Time at address at start (years)[b]	n.c.	10.172	n.c.	n.c.
30	Retired at start of period	0.060	0.082	0.000	0.120
31	Other not employed at start	0.041	0.023	0.039	0.042
32	Retired in period	0.013	0.022	0.000	0.025
33	Became nonemployed, other	0.064	0.023	0.085	0.043
34	Became employed in period	0.008	0.004	0.014	0.003

Table 5-1 (cont.)

Var. No.	Variable	Renters (All)	Owners (All)	Renters Head Under 40	Renters Head 40 or More
35	Job change, new status same or higher	0.123	0.072	0.146	0.100
36	Job change, all	0.151	0.091	0.195	0.107
37	Job change, new status lower	0.028	0.019	0.050	0.007
38	(Distance of change)^2 ÷ 10	0.889	1.384	1.296	0.487
39	Change across region boundary	0.007	0.005	0.008	0.006
40	Distance to job, start of period	3.805	4.943	4.236	3.381
41	(Distance to job)^2 ÷ 10	3.982	5.905	5.188	2.794
42	Job outside region at start of period	0.014	0.007	0.014	0.014
–	Estimated number of households	186,842	646,409	92,741	94,101
–	Number of observations	883	3,085	429	454

[a]Means of binary variables represent proportion of the population for which the variable is positive. The population represented includes only those households meeting the requirements for inclusion in the analysis (see text).

[b]At start of two-year period of observation.

n.c.: not calculated.

More than twice as large a proportion of renters had children born in the period of observation; 20 percent compared to 9. A higher proportion of owners experienced a family size decrease (other than family dissolution); 11 percent compared to 5. Both births and decreases reflect the age differences between the tenure groups.

Also as expected, the mean income of owners was much higher than that of renters; $7,600 compared to $5,900.

Minority groups—nonwhites and Puerto Ricans[a]—were nearly three times as large a proportion of renters as of owners; 28 percent compared to under 10. The minority groups were a higher proportion of young renters than of old.

[a]The preponderant part of the minority population, as defined, was black. Nonwhite population in the Philadelphia and Trenton SMSA's in 1960 was 715,677, of which 705,018, i.e., 98.6 percent, were blacks. Puerto Rican population was 24,836, and a small proportion of these were nonwhite. Thus, in the two SMSA's, blacks were approximately 95 percent of the minority population. Statements applying to the minorities, therefore, may be considered with little chance of distortion to apply specifically to blacks.

The black and Puerto Rican groups also suffered similar disabilities in the housing market. Both tended to be segregated in older parts of the urban area, and both had median incomes well below the median for the entire metropolitan population. For nonwhites, the median family incomes in 1959 were $4,291 and $4,655 in the Philadelphia and Trenton SMSA's, respectively. The comparable figures for the total population were $6,433 and $6,707. The Puerto Rican median family income in the Philadelphia SMSA was $3,603. (That item was not reported for Trenton.) It appears more reasonable, therefore, in studying residential mobility to classify Puerto Ricans with nonwhites than with the white majority.[1]

Thus it appears that age was one of the factors leading to low home ownership by minorities.

Regression Models

As stated in Chapter 4, linear regression calculations were used to estimate the influence of a variety of factors on the probability of moving. The analysis was performed for both renters and owners. The results are shown in Table 5-2.[b]

While the list of factors influencing the probability is similar for renters and owners, the effect of any given factor tends, as anticipated, to be much greater for renters. For example, as shown in Table 5-2, the effect of a nonrelative in the household of a renter is to decrease the likelihood of moving by approximately 30 percent. The same factor has a negative effect of approximately 5 percent upon owners. Similarly, the birth of one or more children has double the effect upon the moving rates of renters as it does upon the rates of owners.[c]

Earlier it was stated that the dependent variable estimate ($\hat{y}$) of the regression models indicates the probability of any family's moving within the two-year period of observation. In view of the statistical problems discussed in the preceding chapter, however, it is reasonable to question the validity of the regression analysis. In addition, the R^2 of the models tends to be low, especially for owners. The higher R^2 obtained for owners is 0.0365 (see Table 5-2).

Two approaches have been taken to making an ad hoc evaluation of the models. The first approach is shown in Table 5-3. Each family in the sample was classified according to the $\hat{y}$ value from Equation 1 or 4 in Table 5-2. Then, for 0.1 intervals of $\hat{y}$ between 0.0 and 1.0, and for all cases whose $\hat{y}$ value was over 1.0 or under 0.0, the number and percentage of movers were calculated. The actual performance of both renters and owners conforms closely with the estimated probability of moving. Large divergences occur only in the extreme intervals which contain small numbers of cases.

The other approach is shown in Table 5-4. Both renters and owners have been cross-tabulated; vertically as movers or nonmovers, and horizontally according to the $\hat{y}$ values from Equations 1 and 4 in Table 5-2. For this evaluation, families were split into those cases for which $\hat{y}$ is over and under the mean probability of moving ($\bar{y}$) for the group.[d] The models are treated as discriminant functions which divide each sample into two classes: movers and nonmovers. If the decision rule is that all families for which $\hat{y} \geqq \bar{y}$ are movers, and others are

---

[b]The table shows three equations for renters and two for owners. The purpose of the separate equations is explained below.

[c]The stated percentages are added to or subtracted from the estimated probability of moving. All such statements concerning the impact of any factor should be construed in this additive sense, not a multiplicative sense.

[d]Unweighted sample means were used for the tests.

nonmovers, families in the first and fourth quadrants of both parts A and B of Table 5-4 are correctly placed.[e] (The figures designating correct placement of families by the discriminant function are underlined.) For renters, there were 594 correct designations (67.3 percent of the total) and, for onwers, 1,827 (59.2 percent).

To evaluate this degree of correct prediction, assume that 346 families had been drawn at random from the renter sample, and that those families had been designated as movers. The remaining 535 were designated as nonmovers. The expected number of errors would have been 210 from predicted movers and a similar number from predicted nonmovers (i.e., 60.8 percent of predicted movers and 39.2 percent of predicted nonmovers), for a total of 420 errors and 463 correct predictions. The percentage of correct predictions would be 52.3. That is significantly[f] lower than the 67.3 percent correctly predicted by means of the discriminant function.

For owners, on the other hand, under the simple assumption that all families were nonmovers, the correct predictions would have been 93.2 percent of the total observations. If the cost of a wrong prediction in either direction is equal, the model of moving by owners is far inferior as a prediction model than the simplistic statement, "Owners do not move." The proportion, however, of movers among predicted movers is over two and one-half times as great as among predicted nonmovers, and a chi-square test of the owner distributions is significant beyond the 0.1 percent level. This, and the results shown in Table 5-3, support the contention that the regression models, even in the case of owners, are useful for the analytic purposes at hand.

Another important consideration for both owners and renters is that the discriminant approach in Table 5-4 isolates a group which is less than half of the sample, but which contains well over half of the movers. This approach, therefore, might be highly useful as an adjunct to further research. An investigator interested in exploring the nature of housing demands in more detail, for example, might use models such as these as discriminant models to separate likely movers and nonmovers. More importance would then be attached to the preferences and demands of the likely movers.

Influences on Moving

Age

For renters, age is one of the most significant factors affecting mobility. (See Table 5-2, Equation 1.) Mobility declines with age, but in a curvilinear fashion.

[e]This decision rule designates as movers all those, and only those, whose calculated probability of moving exceeded the group average probability. This has a certain intuitive appeal, but no theoretical statistical justification is claimed for the rule.

[f]As a null hypothesis, the sample was assumed to be a binomial distribution, with 52.3 percent correct predictions. The normal approximation of the binomial distribution was used to determine significance. Significance was beyond the 0.1 percent level.

Table 5-2
Regression Equations: Moving in Two-Year Period, Married Household Heads

Variable Number	Variable[a]	Renters			Owners	
		Equation 1	Equation 2	Equation 3	Equation 4	Equation 5
		Dependent			Dependent	
	Moved in two-year period					
Personal & Family						
01	Age of head at interview	-0.0278***	-0.0315***	Excl.	-0.00106*	Excl.
02	Age^2 ÷ 100	0.0203***	0.0236***	Excl.	—	—
04	2 Persons married 0-19 years at start[b]	—	—	0.0472	—	—
05	2 Persons married 20 years or more[b]	—	—	-0.0920*	—	—
06	3 Persons, including child under 5[b]	—	—	0.149**	—	—
07	3 Persons, including child 5 or over[b]	—	—	—	—	—
08	3 Persons, including other relative than child[b]	-0.248*	-0.205*	-0.301**	0.0200	0.0179
12	Other relative(s) in household[b]	—	—	—	-0.0337**	-0.0348**
13	Nonrelative(s) in household[b]	-0.295	-0.322*	-0.384*	-0.0492	-0.0513
15	Separated or divorced in period	—	—	—	0.210**	0.214**

#		(1)	(2)	(3)	(4)	(5)
16	Marriage dissolved and remarried in period	0.547*	0.532	0.663*	0.424**	0.419**
17	Child(ren) born in period	0.0852*	0.0932*	0.150**	0.0391*	0.0461**
18	Other family size increase	—	—	—	0.0286	0.0285
20	Head nonwhite or Puerto Rican	-0.0423	-0.0414	—	-0.0206	-0.0193
21	Family income ($1,000's)	0.00482	0.00438	—	0.00290**	0.00284**
Housing						
22	Persons per room 0-0.25[b]	—	—	—	0.0349	0.0315
24	Persons per room over 1.0[b]	0.0520	0.121*	0.0785	0.0363	0.0410*
25	2 in 1-2 rooms, or 3 or more in 3 rooms[b]	0.151**	Excl.	0.145**	0.257**	0.255**
26	3 or more persons in 1-2 rooms[b]	0.348**	Excl.	0.353**	—	—
28	Hotel, motel or rooming house[b]	—	—	—	0.311**	0.316**
29	Time at address at start (years)[b]	—	—	—	0.00105*	—
Job and Work Status of Head						
32	Retired in period	0.167	0.182	—	0.0436	0.0350
33	Became nonemployed, other	-0.129*	-0.138*	-0.116*	—	—
34	Became employed	0.244	0.263	0.310	—	—
35	Changed job, new status, same or higher	—	—	—	0.0270	0.0299*
37	Changed job, new status lower	—	—	0.143	-0.0320	—

Table 5-2 (cont.)

Variable Number	Variable[a]	Renters			Owners	
		Equation 1	Equation 2	Equation 3	Equation 4	Equation 5
38	(Distance of change)^2 ÷ 10	–	–	0.00418	–	–
40	Distance to job start of period	0.00821	0.00834	0.00893*	0.00191	0.00208
41	(Distance to job, start)^2 ÷ 10	–0.00136	–0.00146	–0.00145	–0.000381	–0.000411
42	Job outside region at start of period	–	–	–	0.176**	0.176**
–	Intercept	1.0855**	1.1898**	0.2857**	0.0684**	0.0262**
–	R^2	0.1530**	0.1380**	0.1205**	0.0365**	0.0346**
–	Standard error of estimate	0.4537	0.4571	0.4623	0.2476	0.2477

[a]Variables for which coefficients are absent were excluded generally on account of t values below 1.0.

[b]At start of period of observation.

Excl.: excluded a priori (see text).

Significance: *–5 percent
                **–1 percent

(Single-tailed t test for regression coefficients; F test for R^2.)

Table 5-3
Proportion of Movers by Estimated Probability of Moving, Married Renters and Owners

Estimated Probability[a]	Renters				Owners			
	Total	Movers	Nonmovers	% Movers	Total	Movers	Nonmovers	% Movers
Under 0.0	11	0	11	0.0	90	3	87	3.3
0.0-0.099	10	2	8	20.0	2,577	142	2,435	5.5
0.1-0.199	110	22	88	20.0	344	42	302	12.2
0.2-0.299	188	40	148	21.2	49	12	37	24.5
0.3-0.399	179	61	118	34.1	22	9	13	40.9
0.4-0.499	141	65	76	46.1	2	0	2	0.0
0.5-0.599	126	66	60	52.4	1	1	0	100.0
0.6-0.699	60	40	20	66.7	0	0	0	—
0.7-0.799	32	26	6	81.3	0	0	0	—
0.8-0.899	16	15	1	93.8	0	0	0	—
0.9-0.999	6	6	0	100.0	0	0	0	—
1.0 or More	4	3	1	75.0	0	0	0	—
Total	883	346	537	39.2	3,085	209	2,876	6.8

Table 5-4
Application of Models of Moving as Discriminant Functions, Married Renters and Owners

| | Computed Probability of Moving ($\hat{y}$) | |
	$\hat{y} < \bar{y}$	$\hat{y} \geq \bar{y}$
A. *Renters*		
Total	498	385
Nonmovers	373	164
Movers	125	221
Percent movers	25.1	57.4
Correct =	594 (67.3%)	
B. *Owners*		
Total	1,758	1,327
Nonmovers	1,688	1,188
Movers	70	139
Percent movers	4.0	10.6
Correct =	1,827 (59.2%)	

The net effect of a given age difference diminishes with advance in age.[g]

The effect of the age variables was tested further by performing regression analyses with age excluded. Equation 3 in Table 5-2 is the age-excluded model for renters that had the smallest standard error. For test purposes, exactly the same model but with age (variables 1 and 2) added was calibrated and an *F* test was performed. The *F* test was significant well beyond the 1 percent level. The test equation, however, still had a higher standard error than Equation 1. (It included a number of variables whose *t* value dropped to less than 1.0 when age was put into the relationship.) The inescapable conclusion is that, at least for renters, age is itself significant or is a proxy for highly significant factors which are not included in the model.

For owners, on the other hand, age is much less important. The coefficient of age is small and significant only at the five percent level. The quadratic term did not enter the equation. There is no indication, therefore, of a curvilinear relationship.

The contrasting effect of age and the gross mobility differences between

[g]The net effect of increased age, however, does not become positive within the applicable range. The probability of moving reaches a minimum in relation to age at age approximately equal to 135.

The natural logarithm of age was tested in lieu of variables 1 and 2. The substitution led to a slightly higher standard error. Due to the lack of any statistical or nonstatistical justification for assuming a logarithmic relationship, the assumption was rejected.

renters and owners are illustrated by the examples in Table 5-5.[h] The mobility of renters declines sharply with age; that of owners very little. The mobility of owners at any age, however, is much lower than that even of relatively old renters. The commonly observed increase in residential stability with age is compounded both of the greater proportion of owners among older age groups and of the lower mobility of those who continue to rent.

Family Characteristics and Change

Family composition is not closely related to residential movement. Among renters, when age is included as an explanatory variable, family composition is relevant only for one family type—the family of three that includes a relative not a child of the head. Such families were 20 to 25 percent[i] less likely to move than others in the two-year period. Renters with large families that include such a relative, however, do not have discernibly higher mobility than families without "other" relatives.

The negative effect by "other" relatives was anticipated in Chapter 3. It is reasonable to speculate that, in families of three, this relative is generally an aged parent, aunt or uncle of the head of household or of his wife. The older person's

Table 5-5
Probability of Moving Estimated[a] for Selected Examples, Married Heads

| Age | Probability of Moving in Two Years | | Notes |
	Renter	Owner	
25	0.555	0.054	One child under 5; income $5,000.00; owners in home 2 years
25	0.640	0.093	Same as above, but with child born in period
40	0.365	0.041	Two children; income $6,000.00; owners in home 5 years
60	0.215	0.036	Couple alone; income $6,000.00; owners in home 20 years

[a]Estimated from Equations 1 and 4, Table 5-2. Variables that are not alluded to are assumed to be 0.

[h]For purposes of the calculation, family composition and the values of other independent variables were assumed to be such as might be typical for the ages represented. Assumptions of special conditions, such as particularly high or low ratios of persons per room, were avoided.

[i]Thirty percent less mobile in the age-excluded equation.

neighborhood ties and, possibly, age-connected preference for stability would make moving especially costly in nonmonetary terms. The absence of any apparent effect, however, by "other" relatives in larger families is difficult to account for. Any explanation given at this point would be highly speculative.[j]

Among owners, the presence of "other" relatives, regardless of total family size, reduces mobility by more than 3 percent. The coefficient is highly significant. In view of the low average mobility of owners, that implies that owners with other relatives, and with other characteristics implicit in the intercept, are almost totally immobile. For the 40 and 60 year old examples in Table 5-5, the presence of some "other" relative would reduce the probability of moving in two years to under 1 percent.

The presence of one or more nonrelatives appears to reduce mobility by an amount resembling the effect of "other" relatives: 30 percent or more for renters and 5 percent for owners. The similarity, however, probably is deceptive. A couple might be expected to live with relatives other than their children for reasons which are exogenous to the model presented here. The taking in of nonrelatives is an alternative to moving from a dwelling that otherwise would be too large for the family's demands. While the presence of nonrelatives is treated here as an independent variable, the direction of causality is ambiguous. A desire not to move may account for the presence of roomers, not roomers for the lack of movement.

The exclusion of age from the renter equation alters the apparent effect of family composition. The coefficients of the variables for family composition that enter Equation 3, but not Equations 1 and 2, indicate that those variables may act in part as proxies for age. On the other hand, such variables do indicate stages in the family life cycle which are structurally related to residential mobility.

In Equation 3, families with one small child are shown to move significantly more than the unspecified group. The difference is 15 percent. Such families are at the start of the period of child rearing. The relevant hypothesis advanced in Chapter 3 is that they are moving to housing they consider more suitable for child rearing than the homes they occupied at the start of the period of observation.

The heads of families of two, married 0-19 years, cover a wide range. They are younger on average, however, than all family heads in the sample. Many are young enough to anticipate children,[k] and that may help to account for the

---

[j]A conceivable explanation is that in larger families typical situations may include three generations living together, or a married child and spouse living with his or her parents. In such families, the heterogeneity of the family members may account for the lack of apparent effect by the "other" relative; the heterogeneity leads to a level of space demand that significantly exceeds the space typically offered in rented dwellings. The resulting disequilibrium between demand and consumption could counterbalance the stabilizing effect usually associated with "other" relatives.

[k]Glick and Parke state that the estimated median age of mothers at the birth of the last child is 30, while the median age for first marriage by women born in the 1930s was 19.9 years. Hence, most childbearing occurs in the first 10 years of marriage.[2]

positive coefficient of the variable designating couples married under 20 years.

Couples married 20 years or more and living alone are in the most stable phase of the life cycle. Their family size cannot change generally until the family is dissolved. Hence that source of changes in housing demand is barred. That would lead us to expect the negative coefficient which is found.

For owners, the exclusion of age (Equation 5) has little effect on the estimated relationship of family composition to mobility. In both owner equations, the families of three with one child that is five or older (variable 7) are shown to be about 2 percent more mobile than the unspecified group. Other family types show no deviation. The coefficient for the relevant variable is not significant, and it is difficult to attach any interpretation to it. Other family-type variables do not enter the equation.

The birth of a child[1] leads, as anticipated, to higher mobility for both owners and renters. The effect is 9 percent for renters (15 percent in the age-excluded equation) and approximately 4 percent for owners. Owners, with their typically larger dwellings and higher moving costs, are less frequently impelled to move by the arrival of a child. The larger impact for renters is added to an already higher probability of moving in the absence of a birth. (See the first two lines of Table 5-5.)

A family size increase other than a birth, however, appears to raise the mobility only of owners. The effect on the probability of moving is 3 percent.

Family dissolution by death has no discernible effect on movement by owners or renters. Divorce or separation increases the mobility of owners. The absence, however, of discernible effects from divorce or separation by renters, and from death of a spouse, is not conclusive. As was stated in Chapter 2, coverage of family dissolution by the Supplemental Home Interview may have been extremely weak.

Dissolution of a marriage by any means, combined with remarriage in the two-year period, has, as might be expected, a very large effect on mobility. The combination of events, however, was recorded for extremely few household heads.

Minority families—most of whom were black—appeared to have slightly lower mobility than comparable white, non-Puerto Rican, families. The difference was 4 percent for renters and 2 percent for owners. (In the age-excluded equation for renters, the estimated difference disappeared.) While the coefficients are not statistically significant, they do point in the opposite direction from statements based on a simple interracial comparison. At the least they fail to support the hypothesis of greater mobility by blacks.

Family income has a positive effect on mobility. In the case of owners, the effect although small is significant at the 1 percent level. The effect for renters is a little larger, but in relation to the mean mobility of renters, it is small and

---

[1]The adoption of an infant would also be designated by variable 17. The variable recorded the materialization of a child of the appropriate age during the period of observation.

not significant. The income variable does not enter the renter age-excluded equation. To illustrate the effect, a $5,000 income difference would raise the expected mobility of renters by 2.4 percent and of owners by 1.5 percent.

The positive coefficient of income might indicate that moving is a luxury. Families with higher income can more readily afford to act upon changes in their housing desires. Income might also be positively correlated with recent income change. In that case, the positive coefficient of income would not indicate a response to income *per se*, but upgrading of housing consumption in response to the change.[m]

Housing

In Chapter 3 it was hypothesized that housing arrangements that were crowded or underutilized by usual standards, and dwellings with too few rooms for conventional separation of functions, would lead to higher mobility. Conventional separation of functions requires three rooms for a couple—bedroom, living room, and kitchen. Either of the last two could be used for eating. Larger families require four or more rooms to allow the husband and wife to have one bedroom and other family members another.

The lack of sufficient rooms (as defined above) has a large and highly significant effect for both owners and renters. For renters, the effect on mobility is 15 to 35 percent, and for owners it is approximately 26 percent. A ratio of persons per room exceeding 1.0 also adds to mobility, and that condition frequently or usually accompanies a low room count. It also describes crowded housing where the room count exceeds three. Thus, a small dwelling causes mobility to be increased 20 to 40 percent for renters, and nearly 30 percent for owners. A dwelling which is not small, but which is crowded, has considerably less effect.

Equation 2 is an experiment to see if the persons per room ratio can adequately represent crowding.[n] The variables representing low room count were excluded a priori from the model. Otherwise the equation contains the same variables as Equation 1.

In Equation 2, the coefficient of "persons per room over 1.0" is substantially larger (12 percent) than in Equation 1, and it is significant. But the standard error of Equation 2 is significantly greater than that of Equation 1. A low room count does have a significant independent effect on mobility.[o]

A low ratio of persons per room raises the mobility of owners. A home with

---

[m]It is implicit in this speculation that mean or median income change in the relevant period was positive, or that there is an upward ratchet effect in housing consumption. The responses of owners to job change tend to support the latter implication.

[n]A similar experiment was made for owners. The results were comparable.

[o]An F test was used to compare Equations 1 and 2. Significance exceeded the 1 percent level.

eight or more rooms for two people (which is implied by a person per room ratio of 0.25 or less), and proportionally larger for larger families, may seem both extravagant and undesirable to most families. Such low ratios may be the result of earlier decreases in family size. If so, the resulting higher mobility may be considered a lagged reaction to the decrease.

For renters, however, a low ratio was not found, in earlier versions of the model, to have a significant effect. Fewer than 2 percent of the renter sample had a ratio of 0.25 or below, as compared to nearly 4 percent of the owner population.

Resident owners of motels, hotels, and rooming houses, contrary to expectations, showed much higher mobility than other owners. It was thought that the combination of business and residential ties would lead to high stability. The number of families involved, however, is small and the finding of small importance.

The mobility of owners appears to rise with time in a given home at the rate of 1 percent per decade. The passage of time may lead to an accumulation of small disequilibriums between housing demand and consumption. Such disequilibriums slowly increase mobility, but are not separately represented in the model. The effect of the accumulation is to offset the stabilizing effect of age. In the equation with age excluded, Equation 5, "time at address at start" does not appear. The two variables are positively correlated.[p]

Job Changes and Work Status

The effects of changes in work status (e.g., retiring) and of job changes differ markedly between owners and renters. The effect of job changes on renters, moreover, is ambiguous. Variables representing job changes by renters appear only in the equation with age excluded (Equation 3).

Entering retirement increases the mobility of both owners and renters; owners by 4 percent and renters by 17 percent. For renters, however, the effect does not appear in Equation 3, where age is excluded. For them, the act of retiring counteracts the stabilizing effects of age, and its effect is apparent only when age is taken into account. Since age has less effect on the mobility of owners, the effect of retiring appears to be about the same in Equations 4 and 5. Whether the effect of retiring (for owners and renters) is due to the effect of income change on housing demand, the elimination of job location as a residential location consideration, or both, cannot be determined from the data.

Transition for working to nonworking status other than retired[q] reduces the

---

[p]It is reasonable to ask if, in Equation 4, the estimated coefficients of variables 1 and 29, "age" and "time at address . . . ," respectively, are spurious and the result of collinearity. To test this hypothesis, an equation resembling Equation 4 except for the prior exclusion of variable 29 was calibrated. The coefficient of age remained significant at the 5 percent level.

[q]This includes unemployment as conventionally defined, unemployment due to sickness, and becoming a housewife or student.

mobility of renters by approximately 13 percent. The coefficient is significant at the 5 percent level. That is the opposite of the expected effect. Loss of a job might be expected to lead to retrenchment in consumption and, hence, a move to a less expensive dwelling. A plausible explanation of the observed behavior is that being nonemployed is seen as a temporary status, and families are reluctant to make any binding consumption decisions on the basis of the cessation of employment. They may want to see what their long-term income will be before moving. An unemployed head of household also might be expected to use his energies to search for a new job rather than for a new residence. Where the cessation of employment was due to illness, a residential move would be much more costly than usual, in terms of personal effort. That, too, might help to account for the reduced mobility.

Becoming employed from prior nonworking status[r] increases the mobility of renters by over 24 percent. As with retirement, it is not possible to separate the income and job location effects. It is plausible that what is seen here is mobility that was deferred at the time of becoming nonemployed. With the commencement (or recommencement) or employment, a new income level is confirmed as a long-term prospect, and that level might be much different from the one at the last job.

For owners, neither becoming employed nor becoming nonemployed (other than retired) has any discernible effect. Both events are less frequent for owners than for renters. Becoming employed, especially, was recorded for very few owners.

Job changes were classified according to the change in job status rating which accompanied them. In earlier work with the data, it was found that job changes with no status change, and those with a status rise, had almost identical effects. Those two types of change were combined, therefore, and represented by a single dummy variable. It may be that job changes without status change do typically result in income gains, and by that token have similar effect to job changes with increases in status rating.

Looking at renters, only Equation 3 contains any variables pertaining to job change. One purpose, however, of experimenting with equations which excluded age was to see more clearly the relationship between job changes and moving. Labor force mobility, like residential mobility, is correlated negatively with age.[3] Age might be the ultimate cause both of reduced residential mobility and reduced job mobility. It is still reasonable to suppose, however, that job moves are a proximate cause of residential moves. The close correlation of age with the two types of mobility might, in Equations 1 and 2, obscure a valid relationship between job and residential movement by renters.

---

[r]The event of becoming employed was recorded only for a small proportion of the cases. It may have occurred more often than it was recorded. The SHI did not record work statuses (other than status at time of interview) which lasted less than four months. If a person was not employed two years before the interview, but the total period of nonemployment was under four months, the nonemployed status would not have been recorded. In such cases, a change of job would be indicated rather than the event of becoming employed.

In Equation 3, it appears that any job change increases residential mobility somewhat by virtue of the impact on commuting. Distance of job change, squared, has a small positive coefficient.[s] The effect of a 10-mile change would be to increase mobility 4 percent, of a 5 mile change, 1 percent.[t] A reduction in job status in connection with the change appears to increase mobility substantially, approximately 14 percent. A possible interpretation of the latter is that the income change accompanying status reduction requires moving to reduce housing outlays.

For owners, a job change, with the new job having the same or higher status than the old, raises mobility by 3 percent. Owners appear to respond to the status and income gains implicit in such a job change. The hypothesis of Leslie and Richardson, that families move in response to career status change, appears, at least for owners, to be supported.[4] It seems unlikely that the moves are a response to commuting considerations. The distance of the job change has no discernible effect on owners' mobility.

A job change with reduction in status appears to cause owners to reduce mobility by approximately 3 percent. The coefficient is not significant and appears in only one equation (Equation 4). Even so, it is interesting that the same event appears to increase the mobility of renters.

One's home is both a source of social status and an economic asset. The family whose head has had to take a lower status job may be reluctant to make a further status sacrifice by moving to a less desirable home. A more tangible consideration is that the sale of a home involves the payment of commission and fees equalling approximately 7 percent of the value of the home,[5] and the costs of the sale might be a much larger percentage of the family's equity in its home. A family that has suffered reduced income from the head's wage or salary might be especially reluctant to make any sacrifice of capital. The capital loss, furthermore, would offset at least part of any saving in monthly costs realized by moving. Inasmuch as a loss of job status causes renters to move more, the cost of selling an owner-occupied home, rather than a desire to hold on to the accustomed home, appears to be the salient consideration.

The immediate effect of commuting changes caused by job changes is small for renters, and there is no such effect for owners. Distance to the job of the head of household at the start of the period, however, has a positive effect on mobility rates. The effect increases less than proportionally with distance. A renter who commuted five miles was 4 percent more mobile than one who lived next door to his work. If he commuted 10 miles, he was 7 percent more mobile. For owners, the comparable mobility differences are 0.9 percent and 1.5 percent.

---

[s]In earlier experiments with the data, both the linear and squared variables for distance of job change were allowed to enter the equation. That led to spurious results which appeared to be the result of collinearity. Of the two variables representing distance, tested one at a time, the squared has greater significance.

[t]It is important to note that no attention was given to direction of work change. A more detailed investigation might yield different results.

If the effect of distance to the job at the start of the period is interpreted as a lagged effect of prior employment changes, the effect of distance from the job is more nearly as anticipated in Chapter 3. The effect is not large or highly significant, but it is in the right direction. The marginal effect of a mile of commuting declines with longer commutes. That also seems reasonable. Longer trips to work typically would be, at least in part, through less congested parts of the urban area. Also, long-distance commuters might be expected to use faster modes of travel.[6] The time cost of commuting, therefore, would increase less than proportionally with increases in length of commute.

Those who worked outside the region at the start of the period of observation may be expected to have commuted for very long distances.[u] Among owners, they had considerably higher mobility.

To test further the effect of job or employment status changes on residential movement, married owners and renters were further divided into subgroups on the basis of job or employment change. For each stratum three subgroups were distinguished and the moving behavior of each analyzed. The subgroups were defined as follows:

1. No change by head of household or job or employment status for three years prior to interview;
2. Head of household changed job or employment status in two-year period of observation;
3. Head of household made such a change in year prior to, but not during, period of observation (i.e., only in third year preceding interview).

The purpose of differentiating the third group was to search for lagged effects of a job or employment change. The number of households and proportions of moves in the three groups are shown for both owners and renters in Table 5-6.

In regard to owners, the first group of job changers did move more than nonchangers; those that changed job or employment status in the third year prior to interview, however, moved less. The difference in residential mobility between (1) those who changed jobs or employment status in the two-year period, and (2) all others, is significant at the 5 percent level. Among renters, both changer subgroups had higher moving rates than nonchangers. The difference between all changers and nonchangers is significant at the 1 percent level. (Significance was determined by means of chi-square tests.)

These comparisons, however, give only limited additional support to the importance of job or employment change for residential mobility. The renters in

---

[u]All home interviews and SHI interviews were with households living within a designated cordon. The cordon area was roughly the urbanized part of the nine counties participating in the Penn Jersey Transportation Study. It did not extend to the regional boundaries in most directions. Jobs in New Castle County, Delaware, and Salem County, New Jersey, were counted as within the region, as well as jobs lying between the cordon and the boundary of the nine-county area.

Table 5-6

Number of Households and Proportion of Movers[a], Married Owners, and Renters, by Job or Employment Status Change

Job or Employment Change	Owner		Renter	
	Number	Movers (Proportion)	Number	Movers (Proportion)
No change	2493	0.065	601	0.363
Change 0-2 years before interview	429	0.091	209	0.445
Change only in 3rd year before interview	163	0.055	73	0.493
All changers	592	0.081	282	0.457
All households (total)	3085	0.068	883	0.393

[a]SHI sample data.

the two changer subgroups are on average approximately six years younger than nonchangers. That accounts for over six percentage points—i.e., approximately two-thirds—of the observed difference. For owners, the higher moving rates of those changing jobs or retiring in the two-year period were already indicated to some degree by the coefficients in Table 5-2. The larger group of job changers (those with a rise or no change in job status) and those retiring were shown there to move more than the intercept group.

An additional test was to calculate regression equations for the subgroups of both owners and renters and examine the reduction in unexplained variance (sum of squares) for significance. Regressions were calculated for the following divisions:

1. All changers vs. nonchangers;
2. Changers 0-2 years preceding interview vs. all others.
3. Changers in the third year preceding interview vs. all others.

The variables allowed to enter the equations were those that entered Equations 1 and 4 in Table 5-2.

The calculation of two regressions results, of course, in reduction of the unexplained variance from a single regression. For renters, however, the reduction in variance in all cases was insignificant at the 5 percent level (F test).[7] For owners only one comparison, the last, was significant at the 5 percent level. Since the smaller subgroup had only nine movers, little if any importance can be attached to its mover equation. Since it had a lower moving rate than nonchangers, moreover, the "successful" test can hardly support a conclusion that job changes lead to a delayed, positive, moving response.

These results agree with those of most investigators, that job changes are not among the principal causes of local residential movement. They contrast strongly, however, with the conclusions of Brown and Kain[8] in their recent analysis. As reported in Chapter 2, Kain and Brown found that, for a sample drawn in the San Francisco Bay Area, job changes had a powerful positive effect upon residential movement. One must conclude that the San Francisco area contains an essentially different population in regard to this question, that geographic and other conditions in that area elicit a different response in conjunction with job change, or both.

Neighborhood Influences

Although residential location was seen by Rossi to be systematically related to residential mobility,[9] no attention was given location or neighborhood characteristics in either the heuristic or statistical model examined here. A simple examination has been made, however, of the geographic distribution of residuals from the regression models. The area within the Penn Jersey Cordon was divided into 164 Data Collection Districts. Households in the two groups examined in this chapter were allocated to the district of residence two years prior to the SHI, and the mean residuals by district were calculated.[v] The pattern of positive and negative mean residuals is shown for renters and owners, respectively, in Figures 5-1 and 5-2. Areas with negative residuals had fewer movers than estimated by the regression models, and those with positive, more.[w]

A regular pattern can be seen in both maps. For renters (Figure 5-1) there is a weak tendency for deviations to be positive near the center of Philadelphia and negative in the outlying parts of the Cordon area. For owners (Figure 5-2), moving rates exceeding those predicated are predominant in the older parts of Philadelphia, in some of the close-in suburbs, and in most of Camden. Average deviations are negative in most of the suburbs. Of the outlying pockets with positive residuals, four contain old cities or boroughs—Chester, Malvern, and Norristown in Pennsylvania, and Mt. Holly in New Jersey.

The patterns made by the residuals imply that, even controlling for a variety of factors, mobility is higher in older residential areas than elsewhere, and that neighborhood characteristics associated with central location, aging, or both account for the difference. The area differentiation appears to be stronger for owners than renters. The relationships thus tentatively[x] indicated would bear further examination.

---

[v]Equations 1 and 4 from Table 5-2 were used.

[w]The maps show the Penn Jersey cordon, or survey, area and are based on calculations by Data Collection District. For the central business districts of Philadelphia, Camden, and Trenton, however, overall means were used as a basis for the maps instead of individual Data Collection Districts. Data Collection Districts with zero or one observation were left blank.

[x]The average deviation figures give only a tentative indication that a relationship exists. For

Summary and Conclusion

In this chapter, the influence of several factors on mobility was considered and calibrated simultaneously. The linear regression models used for that purpose appear, on the basis of ad hoc tests, to be valid. The linear regression approach allows calibrating the independent effect of each factor represented in the equations, while controlling for the other variables thought to influence mobility.

The evidence presented here fulfills many of the expectations set forth in the model in Chapter 3, and derived from past research. The close relationship between moving and the family life cycle was, once again, clearly demonstrated. Mobility is much higher for younger families, provided they are renters, and younger families are more likely than older to be renters. Mobility is further increased by the birth of a child.

The apparent effect of age on mobility may stem largely from the rising income of young couples. That is, age may be a proxy for rate of income change. By contrast, the declining family size and possibly declining income of older families—owners or renters—do not cause mobility to increase. There may be a ratchet effect at work. Families will increase their housing consumption more readily than reduce it.

Home owners, who enjoy lower long-term housing costs for a given level of housing consumption, but who face much higher moving costs, move very little. In this case, however, causality may run in two directions. Ownership is financially incompatible with mobility. It seems likely that that is well known, and, consequently, families buy homes only when they can anticipate stability in their housing demands. Thus, even young owners are much more stable than renters of any age.

Job changes and changes in work status have impacts which in general can be rationalized by reference to their income effects. Commuting considerations connected with these changes appear to have little effect on residential movement. What effect they do have appears to occur with a time lag more often than during the same period of observation as the job move. The effect of distance to job at the start of the period is interpreted as a delayed response to commuting burdens undertaken at an earlier date.

Housing arrangements that diverge sharply from conventional norms in regard to the amount of space have a significant influence on moving rates. Lack of

---

most districts, the average deviations for owners are not statistically significant. A t test was performed, using the calculated standard error for the entire region as the standard error estimate in each district. In most cases the t value is below 1.0. Aggregating to larger areas (Philadelphia central business district, rest of Philadelphia, Camden, Trenton, and suburbs in each state), the only significant positive average deviation, for owners, was found in Philadelphia excluding CBD ($t=1.64$), and the only significant negative one in the New Jersey suburbs ($t=2.43$). The average deviations in these areas were 1.1 percent and -2.6 percent, respectively, of owner households. For renters, the significance levels are even less impressive than for owners.

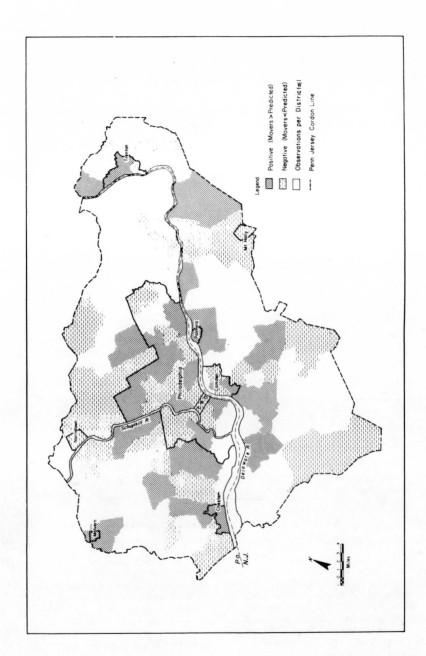

Figure 5-1. Sign of Mean Residual by Small Area, Married *Renter* Mobility Equation.

71

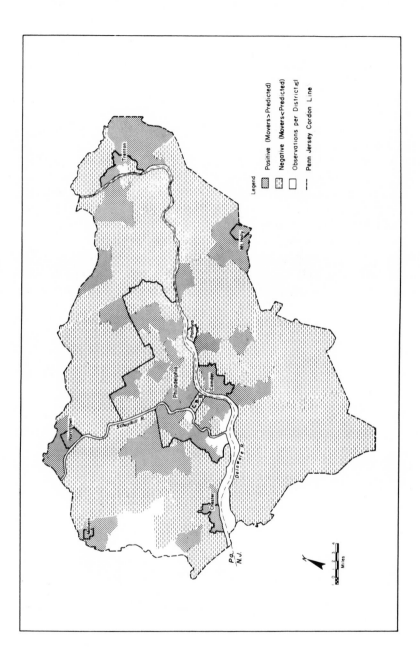

Figure 5-2. Sign of Mean Residual by Small Area, Married *Owner* Mobility Equation.

space for conventional separation of functions is more important than a high ratio of persons per room. A low ratio of persons per room also increases mobility, but only for owners.

Despite the regularities that were found, this examination leaves much to be explained. Even in families in which no event or condition occurs which might tend to increase the probability of moving, the mobility of renters is still quite high, and that of owners is significant. For example, a family consisting of a 40-year-old husband, his wife and two children, living in a four or more room dwelling and not having experienced in the two-year period the birth of a child or a job change by the head of household, has an estimated probability of moving of over 36 percent if renting and 4 percent if they own.

Moving is much less costly for renters than for owners. That helps to account for higher mobility by renters. But even for renters, moving has some costs, and there must be some incentive to move. What incentives might cause families such as the one just described to move is not answered by either the heuristic or statistical models. Many possible explanations beyond those examined here come to mind: for example, income changes, tenant-landlord arguments, destruction of the dwelling, and the desire by many renters for home ownership. Also, the geographic patterns of residuals from the regressions suggests that locational factors influence mobility. Study of the nature and effect of those factors might illuminate not only the mobility of individual families, but also the ways in which the social characteristics of neighborhoods change.

6

Moving by the Unmarried

Unmarried statuses surround the marital family life cycle. That is to say, the term "unmarried" includes both never-married single persons and those persons previously married—i.e., widowed, separated, and divorced. The classification for this study of household heads as married and unmarried depended on the status at the beginning of the two-year period of observation. Some of the unmarried were, not surprisingly, married during the period.

In regard to the unmarried, there are serious gaps in the data. The nature of the SHI is such that household heads who moved out of the region, gave up having their own houshold or died, were lost to the sample. An additional type of loss, which affects only the unmarried subsamples, is that of women who were household heads at the beginning of the observation period, but who married before the SHI was conducted. The survey did not include the histories of former household heads. Despite these losses, results which appear useful have been obtained.

Characteristics of the Groups

Unmarried owners in the sample for this study outnumber renters by just over 30 percent. Among the married, owners are over three times as numerous as renters.

The owner group has a higher proportion of widowed persons—widowers and widows—than the renter group (58 percent compared to 36), and lower proportions of single, divorced, and separated[a] (see Table 6-1). Owners were eight years older on average and had higher average incomes ($5,100 compared to $4,000). Nonwhites and Puerto Ricans were a much higher proportion of renters than of owners (35 compared to 18 percent).

Owners were somewhat more likely to have children (33 compared to 30 percent), but much less likely to have a child under five (1 compared to 8 percent). Average family size of owners was 2.2, as compared to 1.8 for renters. Twenty-two percent of renters lived in one or two room units, as compared to under 1 percent of owners.

On average, unmarried owners had been in their homes a very long time, over 19 years. That is nearly double the figure for married owners, and three to four

---

[a]Separated are grouped with "other" statuses; i.e., with common law marriages and women living with illegitimate children.

Table 6-1

Population Means[a] (Estimated) of Variables Used in Investigation, Unmarried Household Heads

Var. No.	Variable	Renters (All)	Owners (All)	Renters Head Under 40	Renters Head 40 or More
—	Moved in two year period	0.282	0.085	0.497	0.193
01	Age of head at interview	50.661	58.866	31.375	58.566
02	$Age^2 \div 100$	28.156	36.572	10.151	35.537
03	Single at start of period	0.307	0.250	0.468	0.241
04	Divorced at start of period	0.129	0.081	0.134	0.127
05	Separated or other status (not widowed)[b]	0.207	0.088	0.347	0.150
06	Male head of household	0.269	0.285	0.281	0.264
07	Child 0-4 present at start[b]	0.077	0.010	0.221	0.018
08	Child 5 or over present[b]	0.274	0.335	0.350	0.243
09	Any child present at start[b]	0.298	0.335	0.419	0.248
10	Other relative present[b]	0.122	0.315	0.091	0.135
11	Any relative(s) present[b]	0.389	0.590	0.475	0.354
12	Nonrelative(s) present[b]	0.041	0.054	0.043	0.040
13	2 person family at start[b]	0.204	n.c.	n.c.	n.c.
14	3-4 person family at start[b]	0.127	n.c.	n.c.	n.c.
15	Family size 5 or above	0.058	0.071	0.117	0.034
16	Family size at start of period	1.807	2.200	2.250	1.625
17	Family size at interview	1.831	2.094	2.452	1.576
18	Married or remarried in period	0.038	0.022	0.113	0.008
19	Child(ren) born in period	0.030	0.006	0.095	0.004
20	Family increase other than child	0.010	0.047	0.008	0.011
21	Family size decrease	0.052	0.128	0.022	0.064
22	Head nonwhite or Puerto Rican	0.347	0.182	0.503	0.283
23	Family income ($1000's)	3.951	5.114	4.022	3.923
24	Persons per room over 1.0[b]	0.063	0.008	0.139	0.032
25	Persons per room 0-0.50[b]	0.685	0.842	0.551	0.740
26	1-2 room dwelling at start[b]	0.220	0.006	0.226	0.217
27	1 person in 1 or 2 rooms[b]	0.191	0.006	0.179	0.196
28	2 persons in 1 or 2 rooms[b]	0.022	0.000	0.025	0.021
29	3 or more persons, 1 or 2 rooms[b]	0.006	0.000	0.022	0.000
30	3 or more persons, 3 rooms[b]	0.016	0.004	0.035	0.009
31	Rents S-F or owns M-F dwelling[b]	0.216	0.116	0.228	0.211
32	Hotel, motel or rooming house[b]	0.056	0.001	0.072	0.050
33	Time at address at start (years)[b]	6.448	19.224	3.389	7.702
34	Retired at start of period	0.137	0.205	0.000	0.195
35	Other not employed at start[b]	0.228	0.228	0.274	0.209

Table 6-1 (cont.)

Var. No.	Variable	Renters (All)	Owners (All)	Renters Head Under 40	Renters Head 40 or More
36	Retired in period	0.028	0.024	0.000	0.039
37	Became nonemployed, other	0.034	0.020	0.061	0.023
38	Became employed in period	0.014	0.012	0.028	0.007
39	Changed job, new status same	0.036	0.036	0.074	0.021
40	Changed job, new status higher	0.009	0.004	0.018	0.005
41	Changed job, new status lower	0.024	0.008	0.043	0.016
42	Distance of job change	0.362	0.326	0.602	0.264
43	(Distance of change)^2 ÷ 10	0.415	1.157	0.758	0.274
44	Persons per room[b]	0.549	0.367	0.665	0.502
45	Distance to job[b]	2.369	2.246	3.291	1.992
46	(Distance to job)^2 ÷ 10	4.282	4.100	8.242	2.659
47	Job outside region at start[b]	0.000	0.002	0.000	0.000
	Estimated no. of households	105,030	141,785	30,536	74,494
	No. of observations	528	702	158	370

[a]Means of binary variables represent proportion of the population for which the variable is positive. The population represented includes only those households meeting the requirements for inclusion in the analysis (see text).

[b]At start of two-year period of observation.

n.c.: not calculated.

times the figure for the two renter groups.[b] The long period of residence, the high average age of owners, and the high proportion of widowed in the owner group, indicate that many of the unmarried owners are in homes purchased while they were married. The low propensity of unmarried people to buy homes when moving, discussed in Chapter 7, also supports that contention.

Tenure and Mobility

Unmarried home owners move much less frequently than unmarried renters. In the period of observation, just under 9 percent of the owners moved, as compared to 28 percent of the renters (see Table 6-1). The spread is, however, distinctly less than it was for married couples. Thirty-nine percent of married renters and between 6 and 7 percent of married owners moved in the same period.

[b]On average, the married renter subsample had lived in their dwellings 4.9 years at the start of the period of observation. In practice, unweighted sample means are close to the weighted population means shown in Tables 5-1 and 6-1.

Since unmarried renters are on average approximately eight years older than married renters, they might be expected to move less. Unmarried owners move more often than married, however, despite a similar age difference of 10 years. Evidently, home ownership does not provide as stable an arrangement for the unmarried as it does for the married.

Quite possibly, the greater mobility of unmarried owners results from owning homes which were acquired when they were married. After the termination of the marriage, from death or any other cause, the home which was bought during marriage is less appropriate. In particular, the demand for space would be less. The dissolution of a marriage through death was not seen in Chapter 5 to be an immediate cause of moving, and not all heads move after divorce or separation. A lagged effect, however, is possible. After the dissolution of a marriage, the spouse who retains the home might, for emotional or other personal reasons, require more time than is encompassed in the two-year period of observation to make and carry out a decision to move.

Regression Equations

As with the married, regression equations were calibrated for owners and renters to estimate the effect of a variety of factors on mobility. For both tenure groups equations were calibrated both with age allowed to enter and with age excluded a priori. The equations for renters and owners (Table 6-2) are quite different.

Table 6-2

Regression Equations[a]: Moving in Two-Year Period, Unmarried Household Heads

Var. No.	Variables	Renters		Owners	
		Equation 1	Equation 2	Equation 3	Equation 4
—	Moved in two year period	Dependent		Dependent	
Personal and Family					
01	Age of head at interview	−0.0248**	Excl.	−.00255*	Excl.
02	(Age of head)^2 ÷ 100	0.0162**	Excl.	—	Excl.
03	Single at start of period[b]	−0.0735*	—	−0.0476*	−0.0337
04	Divorced at start of period[b]	—	—	0.0812	0.0886*
06	Male head of household	0.0625	0.0601	−0.0363	−0.0379
07	Child 0-4 present at start[b]	—	0.233**	—	0.119
11	Any relative(s) present[b]	—	—	−0.0262	—
12	Nonrelative(s) present[b]	0.188*	0.178*	−0.0676	−0.0524

Table 6-2 (cont.)

Var. No.	Variables	Renters Equation 1	Renters Equation 2	Owners Equation 3	Owners Equation 4
13	2 person family at start[b]	0.119**	0.117**	–	–
14	3-4 person family at start[b]	0.123*	0.156**	–	–
18	Married or remarried in period	0.252**	0.491**	0.137*	0.155*
19	Child(ren) born in period	−0.191	−0.166	–	–
21	Family size decrease	–	–	0.0619*	0.0612*
22	Head nonwhite or Puerto Rican	–	0.0829*	–	–
23	Family income ($1,000's)	–	–	0.00451*	0.00360*

Housing

Var. No.	Variables	Renters Equation 1	Renters Equation 2	Owners Equation 3	Owners Equation 4
24	Persons per room over 1.0[b]	0.196*	0.195*	0.377**	0.382**
26	1-2 room dwelling at start[b]	0.0667	0.640	0.187	0.160
30	3 or more persons in 3 rooms[b]	0.272*	0.285*	0.338*	0.393*
31	Rents single-family house[b]	0.0925*	0.0926*	–	–
32	Hotel, motel or rooming house[b]	0.137	0.204**	–	–
33	Time at address (years)[b]	–	−0.00505*	0.000942	–

Job and Work Status

Var. No.	Variables	Renters Equation 1	Renters Equation 2	Owners Equation 3	Owners Equation 4
34	Retired at start[b]	–	−0.0795	0.0700*	–
35	Other nonemployed at start[b]	0.0715	–	0.0559*	–
36	Retired during period	0.171	–	–	–
38	Became employed in period	–	–	0.308**	0.326**
39	Changed job; new status same	–	–	0.153*	0.127*
40	Changed job; new status higher	0.372*	0.391*	–	–
41	Changed job; new status lower	−0.200	−0.160	–	–
42	Distance of job change	–	–	0.0102[c]	0.0137
43	(Distance of Change)^2 ÷ 10	–	–	−0.00259	−0.00326*
45	Distance to job, start of period[b]	0.00556*	0.00666*	0.00612	–
46	(Distance to job)^2 ÷ 10	–	–	−0.00102	–
–	Intercept	0.9583**	0.1361**	0.1698**	0.0584**
–	R^2	0.2395**	0.1995**	0.0958**	0.0867**
–	Standard error of estimate	0.4071	0.4173	0.2761	0.2763

[a]Equations contain the maximum number of variables for which $t > 1.0$, subject to restraints described in text and below.

[b]Start of two year period of observation.

[c]The t value of this coefficient is below 1.0, but the combined effect of variables 42 and 43 is to reduce the standard error.

Excl.: excluded a priori from the equation.

*Significant at 5 percent.

**Significant at 1 percent.

(Single-tailed t test for regression coefficients; F test for R^2.)

There are important differences in the list of variables which enter the equations, in the size of coefficients for variables that enter both groups' equations, and even in the signs of coefficients for some variables. In addition, some of the coefficients are difficult or impossible to rationalize.

Given these difficulties, there is even more reason to test the validity of the regressions for the unmarried than for the married. The same ad hoc tests were performed for the unmarried groups as for the married. The results, shown in Tables 6-3 and 6-4, support the validity of the equations. (The tests were based on Equations 1 and 3 in Table 6-2.) The proportion of households that moved conforms closely to the predicted probability of moving (Table 6-3), and the discriminant analysis shown in Table 6-4 identified a part of each subsample which contained a significantly higher proportion of movers than did the remainder.[c] The discriminant analysis also made a significantly higher proportion of correct predictions of behavior by renters (71.4 percent) than would have been expected from a random prediction procedure (58.1 percent).

Influences on Moving

Age

The effect of age follows almost the same pattern for the unmarried as it does for the married. Age is highly significant for the renters and is significant at the 5

Table 6-3
Proportion of Movers by Estimated Probability of Moving, Unmarried Renters and Owners

Estimated Probability	Renters				Owners			
	Total	Movers	Nonmovers	% Movers	Total	Movers	Nonmovers	% Movers
Under 0.0	14	2	12	14.3	44	1	43	2.3
0.0-0.099	89	6	83	6.7	439	24	415	5.5
0.1-0.199	103	13	90	12.6	164	19	145	11.6
0.2-0.299	108	26	82	24.1	28	5	23	17.9
0.3-0.399	65	21	44	32.3	13	8	5	61.5
0.4-0.499	56	25	31	44.6	8	3	5	37.5
0.5-0.599	28	11	17	39.3	6	3	3	50.0
0.6-0.699	28	21	7	75.0	0	0	0	—
0.7-0.799	20	16	4	80.0	0	0	0	—
0.8-0.899	8	8	0	100.0	0	0	0	—
0.9-0.999	7	7	0	100.0	0	0	0	—
1.0 or More	2	2	0	100.0	0	0	0	—
Total	528	158	370	29.9	702	63	639	9.0

[c]Chi-square tests were significant at the 0.1 percent level.

Table 6-4

Application of Models of Moving as Discriminant Functions, Unmarried Owners and Renters

	Computed Probability of Moving ($\hat{y}$)	
	$\hat{y} < \bar{y}$	$\hat{y} \geq \bar{y}$
A. *Renters*		
Total	313	215
Nonmovers	266	104
Movers	47	111
Percent movers	15.0	51.6
Correct =	377 (71.4%)	
B. *Owners*		
Total	441	261
Nonmovers	422	217
Movers	19	44
Percent movers	4.3	16.9
Correct =	466 (66.4%)	

percent level for owners. The effect is quite small for owners, approximately 0.3 percent per year, and appears to be linear. For renters, the effect is curvilinear; the net absolute effect of an additional year declines with age. The minimum estimated probability of moving in relation to age is reached between ages 70 and 71. While it is unrealistic to think of mobility increasing after age 70, that aberration is not particularly important for the analysis.

The combined effect of age and tenure can be seen clearly in Table 6-5, which contains the estimated probability of moving for a few hypothetical examples. The assumed ages lie between 25 and 70, and several marital statuses are represented. For each example a family composition and other circumstances which are thought to be compatible with the age and the marital status were assumed. While the estimated probabilities reflect several influences, the effect of tenure and—at least for renters—of age stand out. The effect of tenure, however, tends to disappear for the elderly. For those in their sixties, the estimated probability of moving is similar for owners and renters.

Marital Status

Single (never married) household heads tend to move less than those in other marital statuses. For renters, the difference shows up only in the equation with age included (Equation 1). For renters, the effect of being single is to cancel out in part the influence of age. Single renters are younger on average than other unmarried renters. They form nearly double the proportion of heads under 40 as they do of heads aged 40 or more (see columns 3 and 4 of Table 6-1).

Table 6-5
Selected Examples of Probability of Moving, Calculated from Regressions[a]

Age, Sex, Marital Status	Probability of Move		Notes
	Renter	Owner	
25			
Male, single	0.456	n.c.	5 miles to job.; lives alone
Same—married	0.708	n.c.	
Female, single	0.394	n.c.	5 miles to job; lives alone
Same, with roommate	0.582	n.c.	
Female, divorced	0.586	0.214	One child, under 5. 5 miles to job; income $5,000[b]
40			
Male, single	0.242	0.044	5 miles to job; income $6,000; lives alone
Female, single	0.180	0.080	5 miles to job; income $6,000; lives alone
Female, divorced	0.376	0.183	Two children; income $6,000; 5 miles to job
60			
Widow	0.081	0.082	Income $4,000; 5 miles to job; lives alone
70			
Widow	0.087	0.089	Not working; lives alone; income $3,000
Widower	0.078	0.067	Retired; lives alone; income $3,000

[a]Equations 1 and 3, Table 6-2. Variables that are not alluded to are assumed to be 0.
[b]Income includes pensions and support payments from former husbands, where applicable.
n.c.: not calculated.

Single owners are extremely stable. Their probability of moving is approximately 3 to 5 percent less than that of other unmarried owners. Divorced owners, on the other hand, have higher than average mobility. The coefficient is close to 9 percent in Equation 4 and is significant at the 5 percent level.

The hypothesis advanced earlier, that those who were formerly married find themselves with homes or apartments which are no longer appropriate for their demands, may explain the mobility differences between marital statuses. The single by definition have not experienced any disequilibrating change in status. A divorce, on the other hand, would tend to alter a family's housing demands radically and unexpectedly. The family is split into two smaller segments, each requiring a residence. Widowhood, or widowerhood, does not appear to trigger as strong a mobility response, nor does separation. The tentative nature of separation may restrain the spouse who stays in the family home from making an adjustment and, hence, cause intermediate moving rates for the separated. That is, a separated person may hesitate to make a housing adjustment before entering a more permanent status.

Sex

Moving rates vary by sex of head in opposite directions for renters and owners. Male renters move 6 percent more than female, other things equal. Male owners, on the other hand, have a 3 to 4 percent lower rate of moving. The coefficients, however, are not significant.

One thing indicated by the coefficients for sex is that the difference in mobility between owners and renters is greater for men than for women. Ownership is more economical for those who can remain in one home, and rental for those who must move often. The association of sex and moving rates implies, therefore, that unmarried men are more able than women to benefit financially from their tenure status. The reason for this is not apparent.

Family Composition

Family composition has, like sex, different effects upon the moving rates of owners and renters. It is easier to account for the effect on owners than on renters. The presence of any relative or relatives reduces the mobility of owners by approximately 3 percent. The effect appears only in the equation which includes age. The dummy variable indicating presence of a relative is negatively correlated with age, indicating that there is a greater likelihood of there being a dependent in the household of a younger owner than of an older one. The presence of a dependent seems, therefore, to offset the tendency of younger owners to move more than older.

The lower mobility of families with dependents was anticipated in the heuristic model (Chapter 3). It is more difficult for them than for a lone individual to move. Another possibly contributing factor is that the larger family is more likely to demand the typically larger amount of space found in owner-occupied housing.

Size of family has a large and statistically significant effect upon the mobility of unmarried renters.[d] The relationship is in the form of an inverted-U. Families of two to four persons have a moving rate which is approximately 12 percent above that of larger families or of primary individuals.

It is easy to understand why large families, those with five or more members, would move less than smaller families. Taking care of four or more dependents from day to day poses a large demand upon the energy of an unmarried head of household; to get that many people moved would be especially difficult. There is, however, no apparent reason why a renter without dependents should be less mobile than one with one to three.

The presence of children under five appears in the age-excluded equations to increase mobility of renters and owners. The coefficient for renters is significant at the 1 percent level. To some extent, the variable may be a proxy for age. It also may be that the search for a home thought suitable for child rearing helps to account for the higher mobility of younger household heads.

A nonrelative in the household affects unmarried renters differently from every other group. Married households, whether owners or renters, and unmarried owners, have decreased mobility with a nonrelative. They appear to rent unneeded space to roomers so as to reduce their own space consumption and housing cost without moving. Unmarried renters, however, do not behave in this stable, proprietary fashion. Rather, it may be that they have roommates, and that the arrangement is unstable, one of temporary convenience.

Family Changes

For both owners and renters, marriage[e] increases mobility significantly. The estimated effect for renters is 25 percent if age is included in the equation (Equation 1) or 49 percent if age is ignored (Equation 2). For owners, the effect on mobility is estimated as 14 or 15 percent. Apparently, a higher proportion of unmarried owners consider their dwelling acceptable after marriage. Also, the higher cost of moving for owners would encourage compromise and adaptation.

The birth of a child, which is quite rare among the unmarried[f], decreases

---

[d]The variables for family size of two, three, or four were not present in the original list of variables developed for analyzing moving behavior by the unmarried. The early experiments with the data indicated, however, that for renters the family size was significant in the manner illustrated in Equation 1. The variables were then developed and tested, with the results shown. When the family size variables are brought into the model, the variables which specify family composition in terms of type of dependent lose their significance. For owners, on the other hand, there was no indication that family size per se was significant. The variables for family size of two to four, therefore, were not developed for owners.

[e]Getting married could only be recorded for male heads. Since the SHI histories were taken only for heads of households, the history of a woman would be unavailable if she was married at the time of interview.

[f]Three percent of renters and under 1 percent of owners experienced a birth in the period of observation.

renters' mobility by 17 to 19 percent. It is possible that the apparent effect is spurious. The variable representing a birth of a child or children is highly correlated with marriage in the period, and marriage has a positive estimated effect upon mobility.

Family size decrease causes a significant increase, 6 percent, in the mobility of unmarried owners. The reduction in size may be thought to lead to a lower demand for space and hence to a move. Married owners, by way of contrast, did not show a direct response to a size decrease.

Race and Income

Race appears to have no influence upon the mobility of the unmarried. Race comes only into the age-excluded equation for renters (Equation 2), where it has a coefficient of 8 percent. Nonwhite and Puerto Rican renters are younger on average than white renters. They are approximately twice as numerous among heads less than 40 years old as they are among the older heads (see columns 3 and 4, Table 6-1). It would appear, therefore, that race comes into Equation 2 as an age proxy.

These data help to explain, however, the higher mobility of nonwhites taken as a whole. Given the same circumstances and age, nonwhites and whites have similar rates of movement; among married families, nonwhites have slightly lower rates of moving. They are more heavily represented, however, among young renters, whether married or unmarried, than they are among either older renters or owners. Tenure and age seem to be the principal factors accounting for the difference in average mobility.

The income of owners has a small effect which is significant at the 5 percent level. For each $1,000 difference in annual income, mobility is increased by approximately 0.4 percent. As with married couples, higher income apparently enables unmarried owners to afford the luxury of adjusting their housing to their desires.

Housing

For both renters and owners, crowding has a large and significant effect upon the probability of moving. If the ratio of persons per room exceeds 1.0 at the start of the period, renters are approximately 20 percent and owners 38 percent more likely to move than if the ratio is lower. In addition, if three or more persons are living in three rooms, the probability of moving is increased approximately 28 percent for renters and 34 to 39 percent for owners. A one- or two-room dwelling also has a positive effect upon moving, regardless of the number of people in the dwelling.

Renters of single family houses are approximately 9 percent more mobile than renters of units in multifamily structures. For married renters this distinction has no effect. Possibly the single family houses occupied by the unmarried were originally taken while these people were married. After the termination of the marriage, the occupants tend, with some lag, to move out of these houses and, presumably, into smaller dwellings.

For renters, residence in a hotel, motel, or rooming house also increases mobility. In the age-excluded equation the effect is approximately 20 percent, and is significant at the 1 percent level. Since such quarters are typically rented for a week or a month at a time and often are furnished, it is easy to move out on short notice, and the cost of moving is low. Such dwellings might be expected to attract people who anticipate high moblity.

The number of years of residence at an address enters the age-excluded equation for renters, and its effect is negative. It may be functioning as a proxy for age. For owners, on the other hand, time at an address has a small positive effect, approximately 0.1 percent per year. It enters the age-included equation only.[g] The positive coefficient might be interpreted in the same manner as for married owners; that is, as a proxy for accumulated small changes in circumstances and the resulting demand for space.

Limited importance should be attached to these contradictory effects of time at an address. The variable appears only in the age-excluded equation for renters and the age-included equation for owners. In the former it substitutes in part for age, and in the latter its effect is to weaken the estimated impact of age. Furthermore, owners and renters start with different mean moving rates. A variable which reduces the estimated mobility of renters and increases that of owners brings the behavior of the two groups together. Perhaps the most important aspect of time at an address is that owners and renters who have lived in their dwellings for several years have more similar movement rates than those who have recently moved. Renters become relatively stable because of long-term attachments, and owners become a little less stable because of accumulated changes in their lives and desires.

Job Changes and Work Status

The effect of job changes upon renters is complicated and appears to be solely income and status related. For owners, the effect is more straightforward and stems, at least in part, from commuting considerations.

For renters, a job change with increased job status rating increases mobility

---

[g]As with married owners, time at an address is positively correlated with age. It is reasonable to suspect, therefore, that its coefficient and the coefficient for age are spurious and are the result of collinearity. The coefficient for age, however, is changed only to a small amount if time at an address is excluded from the equation, and it remains significant at the 5 percent level.

by almost 40 percent, while one with reduced status lowers mobility by approximately 20 percent. A job change without status change has no discernible effect. The distance of job change also has no effect.

Renters who experience an increase in status, and presumably in income, may reasonably be assumed to move to improve their housing. The negative effect of a job change with a decline in status is harder to explain. Married renters in such a circumstance moved more frequently than they did without a job change, presumably in order to reduce housing costs. It may be that the coefficients of this variable for unmarried renters are a fluke. The sign is "wrong," and the coefficients are not significant at the 5 percent level (10 percent with a two-tailed test).

While the response of unmarried renters to job change is unrelated to the distance between old and new jobs, the distance from home to work at the beginning of the period of observation has a significant effect. The impact, approximately 0.6 percent per mile, may be considered a lagged response to the burdens of commuting.

Owners respond to a change of job with increased mobility. The coefficient for change of job with no status change is approximately 15 percent and is significant at the 5 percent level. (Other types of job change occur very rarely, and that may account for their not entering the equation.) The distance of job change also has a positive effect; the marginal effect diminishes with increased distance.[h] The distance to job at the beginning of the period has a similar curvilinear effect upon moving. The response to distance to work resembles that of married owners and married renters. The size of the response is greater for unmarried owners than for married owners and slightly less than it is for married renters.

Owners who were retired at the start of the period, and owners and renters who were in other nonworking statuses, tended to move 6 to 7 percent more frequently than if they had been working.[i] Both variables enter only the age-included equations, but for owners they are significant at the 5 percent level. The reasons for the increased mobility might well be that those not working are less tied by commuting considerations to the location of their current homes. They can move more readily for any reason. Nonworking status did not, however, affect the mobility of married heads of household. Evidently married families are more attached to their homes, whether rented or owned. Unmarried household heads might be expected, for reasons explained above, to be experiencing disequilibrium in their housing adjustment. Where the bonds of work are removed, therefore, mobility is more easily affected than it is for married couples.

---

[h]The t value for distance of change (linear) is below 1.0. But the introduction of the two variables for distance of change reduces the standard error of estimate.

[i]In Equation 2, the age-excluded equation for renters, those who are retired are shown as having lower mobility. The variable appears to be acting in that context as a proxy for age.

For renters, retirement during the period of observation leads to higher mobility, while retired status at the start does not. This may simply indicate that renters respond more rapidly to the income and commuting effects of retirement than do owners.

Finally, to become employed from a previous nonworking status increases the mobility of owners by approximately 30 percent. Despite the rarity of the event, which occurred for 1.2 percent of owners, the coefficient is significant at the 1 percent level. The tendency to move might be viewed as a response to the change in income or to commuting burdens. It also seems plausible, however, to think of both the act of seeking employment and the selling of a home as the response to a single additional factor, financial stringency.

Summary

In this chapter the factors influencing residential mobility of unmarried heads of household were examined. For the unmarried, as for the married, tenure is highly significant. Moving rates are much greater for renters than for owners, but the spread is less than for the married. Unmarried renters move less than married, perhaps due to being eight years older on average. Unmarried owners, however, despite similar age difference, move more than married. Many of the unmarried owners may have bought their homes while married, and that may explain their being more mobile than married owners. Their higher moving rate may be a lagged response to the dissolution of the marriage and the resulting disequilibrium between housing demand and consumption.

That interpretation is supported by the lower moving rates of single heads, as compared to other unmarried heads. Among both renters and owners the single move less.

The effect of age upon the unmarried was similar to the effect upon the married. For renters, it was highly significant and curvilinear. The net effect of an added year declines with age. For owners the effect is less significant and linear.

For both tenure types, crowding of housing is a highly significant factor leading to increased mobility. Renting of a single family home or, at the other extreme, renting quarters in a hotel or similar transient quarters, also adds to mobility. Both of these types of accommodation must be seen as inappropriate, although for different reasons, for long-term residence.

Sex and family composition have effects which vary, between owners and renters, in size and in direction. The differences have not been explained.

Income has a positive effect upon the mobility of owners. Race was found not to be important. The low average age and low proportion of home owners among nonwhites account for the higher average mobility of that group.

Job changes and changes in work status (e.g., retiring or becoming employed) tend to increase mobility. The equations show income and status effects for renters and both those effects and the effect of commuting considerations for owners. The distance to work at the start of the period for both owners and renters has a positive effect upon mobility. Thus, commuting burdens have some lagged effect upon moving for the unmarried, as they do for the married.

7

The Decision to Buy or Rent

In the last two chapters, the residential mobility of households with married and unmarried heads, respectively, has been examined. As expected, tenure was found to be one of the best predictors of mobility. Renters of almost every description are much more mobile than owners, regardless of family characteristics. The chief exceptions are households with elderly, unmarried heads.

While prior tenure was assumed in the last two chapters to be an independent variable, it is reasonable to ask how the tenure of each family was itself determined. It was suggested in Chapter 3 that mobility expectations influence tenure. Because home ownership yields savings in housing cost which, within two or three years, exceed the cost of selling the home, those families which anticipate stability in their residential demands, including locational requirements, tend to purchase. For a shorter period, the transaction cost of selling a home would lead to higher total cost of housing for owners. Consequently, a family which, when moving, intends to move again within a short period is more prone to choose rental housing.

Tenure in the prior residence, family size, income, and race were also hypothesized to affect tenure choice. A former owner would be more likely to have saved the money required for a down payment. Prior ownership would also indicate that the style of living implicit in home ownership was accepted by the family. Large families are more likely to desire the larger dwelling size that typically comes with ownership, while high income provides the means for purchase. Although ownership is less costly than rental for a given size and type of dwelling, renters typically spend less for housing than owners. The difference stems from the average size and quality of rental and sales housing.

Race is expected to influence choice of tenure, although there is no intrinsic reason for it to do so. It was anticipated that nonwhites would be less prone to purchase their homes. In established black neighborhoods and their immediate surroundings, rental units are a higher proportion of the housing stock than in the urban area as a whole. That tends to make the opportunities for purchase by blacks more limited relative to demand than opportunity for rental.

Marital status interacts with most of the factors listed above. Marriage is viewed as a long-term status. At least some of the unmarried, on the other hand, anticipate changed status and, hence, housing needs. That implies residential mobility. Unmarried movers also have smaller average family size and lower income than married, and a larger proportion of the unmarried are nonwhite or Puerto Rican (see Table 7-1). All of these considerations lead toward rental. It is

Table 7-1

Estimated Population Means^a of Variables Used for Regressions: Tenure Choice Problem

Variable Number	Variable	Married	Unmarried
–	Purchased home after move	0.540	0.157
01	Owned prior home	0.333	0.282
02	Nonwhite or Puerto Rican	0.196	0.368
03	Age of head at move	38.426	44.443
04	Age$^2 \div 10$	163.924	219.470
05	Family size at move	3.817	2.236
06	(Family size)$^2 \div 2$	9.016	3.767
07	Family income in \$1,000's	6.773	4.316
08	Income$^2 \div 10$	7.429	3.339
09	Income $\div$ family size	2.198	2.698
10	Relative(s) other than own child in household	0.059	0.147
11	Couple married 0-19 years	0.113	n.c.
12	Couple married 20 years or more	0.102	n.c.
13	Couple with 1 child, married 0-19 years	0.245	n.c.
14	Couple with 1 child, married 20 years	0.000	n.c.
15	Couple with other relative only	0.015	n.c.
16	Number of children at move	1.746	1.047
17	Male head, single	n.c.	0.082
18	Female head, single	n.c.	0.114
19	Male head, other status	n.c.	0.171
20	Female head, other status	n.c.	0.633
–	Number of moves represented	125,801	49,958
–	Number of observations	608	264

^aFor binary variables, the mean is the estimated proportion of movers who possessed the characteristic described. The population is all movers during a two-year period. A family is counted the number of times it moved.

n.c.: not calculated.

not surprising, therefore, that over three times as high a proportion of married movers as unmarried bought a home—54 compared to 16 percent.

Method of Investigation

The method of investigation is the same as that used to investigate mobility. Least squares linear regression was used to estimate the probability of purchasing a home at the time of a move (see Table 7-2). The regression coefficients are

Table 7-2
Probability of Home Purchase, Given a Move: Regression Analysis[a]

Variable Number	Variable	Married	Unmarried
–	Purchased home	Dependent	
01	Owned prior home	0.271**	0.245**
02	Nonwhite or Puerto Rican	−0.157**	–
03	Age of head at move	0.0217**	0.00826
04	Age^2 ÷ 10	−0.00249**	−0.000781
05	Family size at move	0.109**	0.0299*
06	(Family size)^2 ÷ 2	−0.0193**	–
07	Family income ($1,000's)	0.0297**	0.0302**
08	Income^2 ÷ 10	−0.00431**	−0.00591
10	Relative(s) other than own child in household	–	0.225**
17	Male, single	–	0.119
19	Male, other status	–	−0.0724
	Intercept	−0.3622*	−0.3086*
	R^2	0.2182**	0.2878**
	Standard error of estimate	0.4437	0.3177

[a]Each equation contains only those variables which could enter the equation with a t value of 1.0 or greater.   **Significant at 1 percent level.
*Significant at 5 percent level.
(Single-tailed t test for regression coefficients; F test for R^2.)

estimates of the effect of the independent variables on that probability. Each move made by a household was considered a separate observation. As in the investigation of mobility, only households which could furnish two years of continuous history were used. Furthermore, any household whose head was an inmigrant to the region or who had been living in an institutional residence two years prior to the interview was excluded. A separate examination was made for married and for unmarried heads of household. The differences between the two groups are profound enough to justify the division.

In the regressions, the dependent variable was binary in form, with the value of 1.0 representing home purchase and the value of zero representing renting or similar status after the move.[a] The independent variables common to both regressions are age of the head of household at the time of the move, family size, family composition, income, race, and ownership of prior home. The remaining independent variables are family composition for the married, and sex and marital status for the unmarried. The variables for race, prior ownership, marital status, and sex are binary in form, with the value of 1.0 indicating presence of

[a]Renting includes unusual statuses such as living rent free or receiving quarters in connection with a job.

the characteristic represented. Age, family size, and income are scalars. They are represented linearly and by their squares (e.g., income, in thousands of dollars, squared). That makes it possible to investigate the existence of curvilinear relationships. The squared variables are reduced by constants which serve to keep their absolute variances smaller than they otherwise would be. That is desirable for maintaining computational accuracy.

Age was found in the investigation of mobility to be highly significant, especially for renters, as a predictor of movement. It is used here as a proxy for mobility expectations. The relevance of the other independent variables is straightforward, as described above.

The regression results in Table 7-2 conform closely with expectations. Nonetheless, the same ad hoc tests were performed on these equations as in the equations for moving. For this application, too, the tests support the validity of the regression analyses. The proportion of buyers among both married and unmarried tends to conform to the estimated probability of purchase (Table 7-3). In the application of the regression equations as discriminant functions (Table 7-4), a part of each subsample (married and unmarried) was identified which contains under half of the observations, but well over half of the buyers.[b] For the married, moreover, the percentage of correct predictions (70.1 percent) is significantly greater than would have been expected from a random prediction

Table 7-3
Proportion of Home Buyers by Estimated Probability of Purchase, Married and Unmarried Movers

Estimated Probability	Married				Unmarried			
	Total	Buyers	Renters	% Buyers	Total	Buyers	Renters	% Buyers
Under 0.0	4	0	4	0.0	54	0	54	0.0
0.0-0.099	3	0	3	0.0	71	2	69	2.8
0.1-0.199	18	2	16	11.1	40	4	36	10.0
0.2-0.299	63	16	47	25.4	35	9	26	25.7
0.3-0.399	90	27	63	30.0	34	9	25	26.5
0.4-0.499	121	56	65	46.3	13	6	7	46.2
0.5-0.599	91	53	38	58.2	6	2	4	33.3
0.6-0.699	54	40	14	74.1	6	6	0	100.0
0.7-0.799	51	34	17	66.7	3	3	0	100.0
0.8-0.899	63	58	5	92.1	2	2	0	100.0
0.9-0.999	34	31	3	91.2	0	0	0	–
1.0 or More	16	14	2	87.5	0	0	0	–
Total	608	331	277	54.4	264	43	221	16.3

[b]For both married and unmarried, Chi-square tests are significant at the 0.1 percent level.

Table 7-4

Application of Models of Tenure Choice as Discriminant Functions, Married and Unmarried Movers

	Computed Probability of Buying ($\hat{y}$)	
	$\hat{y} < \bar{y}$	$\hat{y} \geq \bar{y}$
A.*Married*		
Total	349	259
Renters	<u>222</u>	55
Buyers	127	<u>204</u>
Percent buyers	36.4	78.8
Correct =	426 (70.1%)	
B.*Unmarried*		
Total	153	111
Renters	<u>148</u>	73
Buyers	5	<u>38</u>
Percent buyers	3.3	34.2
Correct =	186 (70.5%)	

process[c] (50.3 percent). (For the unmarried, more correct predictions would have been made by assuming no one bought.)

Influences on Tenure Choice

Age of Head and Prior Tenure

For both married and unmarried, the probability of purchase increases with age up to a point and then declines. The effect of age is considerably larger for the married, and it is significant at the 1 percent level. For the unmarried it is not significant. The maximum probability of purchase in relation to age for both groups is reached well within the range covered by the data. It occurs at approximately age 44 for married heads of household and 53 for unmarried.

The decline in the probability of purchase at higher ages is compensated, however, by the effect of prior ownership. Prior ownership, which significantly increases the probability of purchase, is more common among older movers than among younger.[d] The effect of the two variables, age and prior ownership, indicate that beyond middle age those who have not yet bought a home become less rather than more likely to do so. Their taste or style of life is such, as to

---

[c]That is, from assuming that 54.4 percent of the sample, drawn at random, were buyers.

[d]For both the married and the unmarried, variable 1, owned prior home, is highly correlated with age.

make home ownership uncongenial. Also, married couples in their middle forties and beyond are in a phase of life in which family size will be stable or declining. They would not, therefore, buy a home in anticipation of further increases in family size.

Table 7-5 shows the estimated probability of purchase for a few selected hypothetical examples. At each of the three ages represented, the married couples, provided they are white, have the highest probability of purchase,[e] and the probability of purchase appears to go up monotonically with age. It does so because of the assumption that the oldest movers had owned their prior home and that the others had not. That assumption, however, is realistic.

Table 7-5
Estimated Probability of Purchase Given a Move, Selected Examples

Age	Situation[a]	Probability
25	Couple, one child, white; income = $5,000	0.403
	Same, black	0.246
	Bachelor alone; income = $5,000	0.134
	Single woman, as above	0.015
40	Couple, 2 children, white; income = $5,000	0.527
	Same, income = $7,000	0.576
	Couple, 2 children, black; income = $5,000	0.370
	Divorced woman, 2 children; income = $5,000	0.123
	Same, with 1 child and "other" relative; income = $5,000	0.348
	Bachelor, alone; income = $5,000	0.182
	Bachelor with "other" relative; income = $5,000	0.437
60	Couple, alone, owned prior home; income = $5,000	0.632
	Same, income = $7,000	0.681
	Widow, alone, owned prior home; income = $5,000	0.319
	Widower, as above	0.246

[a]White, not Puerto Rican, if not specified. Variables not alluded to assumed to be 0.

[e]It is possible for some unmarried persons to have a higher calculated probability than some married. For example, if the couple with two children and 40 year old head were assumed to be black, they would have a lower probability of purchase than the example of a bachelor of the same age with some "other" relative.

Family Size and Composition

With married household heads, family size has a curvilinear effect similar to that of age upon the probability of purchase. The probability of purchase increases with family size up to five or six[f] and then declines. Both coefficients involved (variables 5 and 6) are significant at the 1 percent level.

The lower propensity of very large families to purchase may be due to the effect of family size on the family budget. Food and clothing increase with family size as a proportion of the budget, and housing declines.[1] That may have an effect similar to the effect of lower income as discussed below.[g]

There may also be a threshold effect which causes a decline in the marginal impact of additional family members. When family size is large enough so that the typical apartment is too small by common standards, the propensity to purchase would be quite strong. The presence of additional family members beyond that point can contribute little additional impetus. It might, rather, cause a family to look for a larger home within the sales housing market.[h]

For unmarried heads, the effect of family size is less significant and is linear. An additional family member increases the probability of purchase by approximately 3 percent. If, however, one of those family members is a relative other than a child of the head, the effect is over 25 percent (the sum of the coefficients of variables 5 and 10).

Approximately 15 percent of unmarried movers had some "other" relative in the household. That relative might frequently be an elderly parent who has savings and income with which to assist in the purchase of the home. It is also possible that the attitude towards home and property of unmarried heads with "other" relatives differs from that of other unmarried heads.

Among the unmarried, single men tend to purchase more frequently than women. The difference is approximately 12 percent. Other men, however, have a lower propensity to purchase than women; the difference there is approximately 7 percent. The single men may be moving in anticipation of a marriage. The homes they purchase would then be intended for use by themselves and their intended brides. There is no obvious explanation, however, of the lower propensity to purchase by men in other marital statuses.

---

[f]The calculated value for the size of family which maximizes the probability of purchase is 5.65. A family size of five or of six has an almost identical effect on the estimated probability of purchase (0.304 compared to 0.307).

[g]Larger families, income held constant, have been observed to accept lower quality rather than smaller dwellings.[2] The effect that family size has on the propensity to purchase, therefore, is influenced by the size-quality-tenure distribution of the available housing supply.

[h]The term, threshold, is used loosely here. There is not a sharp demarcation between families large enough to find home purchase desirable and other families. The overlap of the size distribution of rental and sales housing prevents a sharp division. In addition, families live with widely varying ratios of persons per room.

Income

For both married and unmarried heads of household, income has a significant positive effect upon home purchase. The effect is curvilinear and the marginal impact declines with increase in income.[i]

Income may have a threshold effect similar to that described for family size. Few housing units for sale are cheap enough to be bought by families with very low income (under, say, $3,000 in 1959). With increasing income a progressively larger selection of sales housing becomes available. The same, of course, is true of rental units, but the effect is less marked. That is, a higher proportion of the rental housing stock is priced within the means of families in the lowest income groups.

For a family with income sufficient to allow it to purchase new housing, income offers little constraint upon purchase. The supply of new units can be expanded to meet any shift in the demand curve for the purchase of housing. The savings stemming from home ownership, however, continue to rise with income. The income tax bracket of the family will be higher, thereby making the savings from ownership a higher proportion of the pretax cost of housing. Wealthier families may also be expected to demand larger or better housing units, or both, thereby further increasing the expected savings. Hence, the marginal effect of income can be expected to remain positive at higher income levels.

Race

As expected, minority households (predominantly black) are significantly less likely to purchase than whites. The coefficient is close to 16 percent for married families and is significant at the 1 percent level. The variable does not enter the equation for the unmarried.

The implication of lower propensity to purchase by blacks and other minorities is that their opportunities for home purchase were at that time and place more restricted than opportunities for rental. That is, the race premium must have been relatively higher for would-be purchasers than for renters.[j]

---

[i]A maximum estimated probability of purchase in relation to income occurs at approximately $34,000 for married couples and just under $26,000 for unmarried. Those levels exceed the mean income of the groups by several standard deviations, however, and it is probable that there were few, if any, observations of families with income that high or above. To say that the maximums exist empirically, therefore, requires extrapolation beyond the survey data. There does not appear to be any nonstatistical rationale for such an extrapolation. Consequently the speculation that the propensity to purchase reaches a maximum in relation to income and then declines seems untenable.

[j]The premium includes a noncash effect of the locational constraint. Even if a black buyer pays the same amount for a house as a white buyer would for that house, the house and location frequently would be a suboptimal choice in the absence of racial restraints.

Another possible interpretation is that the blacks were poorer than their dollar incomes would indicate. That is simply an alternative way of looking at the housing-cost premium imposed upon them.

Summary

In this chapter, the probability of purchasing a home at the time of a move has been examined. It was hypothesized that the probability of purchase would be higher for the married, and would be increased by age, family size and income. Blacks were expected to purchase less frequently than whites.

The expectations concerning the influence of those variables were fulfilled. Unmarried heads of household were found to have much lower propensity to purchase than married. Among both groups, family size, age, and income were found to have a positive effect upon home purchase. The marginal effect of age and income for both groups, and of family size for married couples, declines with an increase in the variables. In regard to age and family size, it was found that the maximum probability of purchase occurs well within the range of the observed values of the variables. The budgetary impact of large family size may explain that downward turning effect.

The positive effect of prior ownership compensates for the downward turning effect of higher age levels. That is, a larger proportion of older movers in both groups owned the home from which they moved. Prior ownership was found to have a strong positive effect upon the probability of purchasing the new home. It indicates that the life style implicit in home ownership has been accepted previously by the family, and it may also be associated with the accumulation of assets which can be used for a down payment on the next home.

Finally, race was found to have a significant effect upon the probability of home purchase by married couples. Married blacks are approximately 16 percent less likely to purchase than comparable whites. That indicates that their opportunities for home purchase are relatively more restricted than the opportunities for rental.

8

Summary, Conclusions, and
Next Steps

Influences on Mobility and Home Purchase

Life Cycle

The guiding conception of residential movement in this study is that mobility is principally a means of adjusting housing consumption to changes in housing demand. Changes in demand stem from events and stages in the family life cycle, income changes, and events in the head of household's career. Whether a family rents or owns its dwelling also influences mobility (see Table 8-1). Tenure may, in fact, be the most powerful predictor of mobility. The decision, however, to buy or rent when moving is itself partly determined by future mobility expectations. Thus, home ownership and low mobility are mutually reinforcing.

By putting together the findings concerning mobility and tenure choice, it is possible to form a coherent description of residential mobility and tenure during the life cycle of a family. The findings generally confirm the tentative conclusions set forth in Chapter 2, on the basis of earlier research. Young families typically rent their dwellings, and for renters mobility tends to decline with age. The reason for the decline with age was not determined from the data, but it is hypothesized to be that income tends toward a stable level in middle

Table 8-1
Summary of Mobility and Home Purchase

	Families Represented		Movers %	Moves Represented	Proportion Buying (%)
	Number	%			
Married					
Owners	646,409	77.6	6.5	–	–
Renters	186,842	22.4	38.9	–	–
Total	833,251	100.0	13.8	125,801	54.0
Unmarried					
Owners	141,785	57.4	8.5	–	–
Renters	105,030	42.6	28.2	–	–
Total	246,815	100.0	16.9	49,958	15.7

age, and income change is one of the major factors leading to mobility. As family income increases there is a desire to improve housing consumption in terms of space, quality, or both. Specific life cycle events, notably marriage and the birth of a child, also add to mobility.

As the head of the family approaches middle age, the propensity for purchase, given a move, rises steadily. Expected future mobility is low; family income and family size are typically at or near a maximum. All these factors encourage purchase. By buying its home as income approaches a plateau, the family is able to gain an additional increment in income. The gain is in kind, not cash. Minority families are less likely than comparable majority to buy. There is no reason to attribute the difference to factors other than restricted opportunity.

Mobility remains low in the later years of family life. It declines with age, especially for renters, and it is low at all ages for owners. Families continue to occupy housing which was acquired when family size and income were greater. Emotional ties to a family home may contribute to stability, and there may also be a ratchet effect in housing consumption. Older couples who do move have a high propensity, especially if they have owned before, to purchase rather than rent.

Unmarried home owners, the majority of whom are widowed, respond more readily than married to life cycle events. For example, a family size decrease has a determinable effect upon the mobility of unmarried home owners while it has no observable effect upon married. Most of the unmarried owners appear to have purchased their homes when they were married. The subsequent dissolution of the marriage would cause a disequilibrium in their housing consumption, and that, in turn, may account for their greater responsiveness to any later stimulus.

Housing Space and Mobility

Both crowding and a small number of rooms were found to add independently to mobility. That is, families which started the period of observation in dwellings which were small or crowded were more likely to move than others. Small size, as indicated by a low room count, had a more significant effect than a high ratio of persons per room.

It was hypothesized in the heuristic model that when families choose a home, they take into account predictable changes in their demands. Consequently, mobility would be lower shortly after a move than later. Only unanticipated changes in demand, or changes which occur too long after the move to have influenced the choice of housing, lead to a divergence of demand and consumption.

Apparently, only buyers anticipate in this fashion. The mobility of owners does increase with time in the dwelling. The relevant variable appears only in the equations that include age. The effect is to counterbalance in part the negative effect of age on mobility. The substantial cost of selling a home provides incentive for considering future as well as current demands. For renters, on the other hand, the cost of moving apparently is too small to have a noticeable effect. Only immediate considerations appear to guide the choice of rented dwellings.

Marital Status

Unmarried owners are more mobile than married; 8.5 percent of unmarried owners, as compared to 6.5 percent of married, move in two years (see Table 8-1). Higher mobility by unmarried owners is to be expected. As stated above, most unmarried owners appear to have bought their homes when married. With the dissolution of the marriage, their housing demands may be expected to decline substantially, thereby introducing a strong element of disequilibrium.

While dissolution of the family may weaken the ties to the home, that is not evident at the time of change of marital status. On the other hand, it is possible that many surviving spouses in the case of death of the other spouse, and many separated or divorced people, either migrate out of the region or move in with relatives. People who made any of these moves were lost to the survey. The evidence concerning movement at the time of marital status change, therefore, is highly questionable.

Unmarried renters move 11 percent less than married in a two-year period. Approximately 8 out of the 11 percentage points can be attributed to the difference between the mean ages of the groups.[a]

Among the unmarried, the single are relatively stable. For either tenure group, their mobility is lower than that of people in other statuses. That may be because, by definition, the single could not have had a change in marital status which would lead to disequilibrium between their housing consumption and demand.

The unmarried have a low propensity to purchase homes when moving. Their average income and family size are both smaller than those of the married, and that discourages home purchase. A consequence of the high propensity to rent is that the proportion of renters among the unmarried is much higher than among the married. That, in turn, helps account for the higher overall mobility of the unmarried (see Table 8-1).

Job and Commuting

The effects of job change or change in work status on mobility appear to be primarily, although not entirely, income effects. That indirectly supports the

[a]Based upon the coefficients of age in Equation 1 in Table 6-2.

hypothesis that income change is an important cause of residential mobility. The burden of commuting has a small effect on mobility, and the response appears to occur at least in part with a lag after a change of job. Thus, the data give only weak support for traditional urban land rent theory and related theories of urban form. The tradeoff between space costs and accessibility is only one of many factors affecting housing decisions.

Applications

In this investigation, linear probability equations were specified and calibrated which estimate with considerable success the probability of a move and of home purchase given a move. One use of analysis of the type presented here would be in housing market studies. Such models could be used to determine which types of family were more likely than the average to be actively in the housing market, and to separate those families into probable purchasers and renters.[b] Using that information, a researcher could achieve considerable economy by concentrating his attention upon those who are likely to be in the market in which he is interested.

Another application, mentioned in Chapter 1, is in modeling metropolitan growth and form. The urban simulation models undertaken by the Penn Jersey Transportation Study and the National Bureau of Economic Research require submodels to identify active demanders of sales and of rental housing.[1] The Penn Jersey effort described above has not led to significant published findings, and the National Bureau model is not fully operational for its intended uses. But the approach of first estimating the number and characteristics of movers, and then examining their locational choices, offers promise of leading around one of the knotty problems in modeling urban form—i.e., the problem of the immobility of households and the effect of that immobility on patterns of residential distribution. At least one study of nonresidential location patterns also follows this general approach.[2]

Leaving the subject area of this study, the methodology offers potential for widespread application. In Chapter 1, a few examples of problems that lend themselves to discriminant or probability analysis were cited. The method is in fact applicable to virtually any problem in which phenomena of interest fall into two distinct and mutually exclusive classes. Such problems can arise in connection with housing stock change, educational programs (success of participants), migration, municipal bond referendums, or industrial location, to mention a few.

---

[b]The equations would have to be reformulated to include as independent variables only information that is knowable a priori.

Desirable Future Research

Survey Requirements

The data source used for this study is extraordinarily rich in relevant detail. It does, however, have some shortcomings for the research at hand. The most important omission for the study of mobility and home purchase is income change. Ideally, income change should be determined not only over the period during which housing actions are observed, but also for a few years beforehand. That is, the income history should be long enough to allow studying lagged reactions to change in income. If income change data were available, it would be possible to determine with more confidence than is now possible if age is functioning as a proxy for income change. Age is, of course, directly observable and predictable. If it is a reliable proxy for income change, it can be used in models with reasonable confidence in the stability of the relationships involved.

The accumulation of savings is of similar importance to income change. Home purchase requires a lump-sum payment which even under the liberal rules of FHA financing is substantial. The various fees required for property transfer, such as title search and insurance charges, are included in that initial payment.

A 12-year family history, however, is not necessary for housing research. Good results were obtained here using only two years of the Supplemental Home Interview histories. The shorter period may, indeed, have some advantages over an extended history. There are fewer erroneous responses caused by memory lapses, and a shorter history introduces less bias from out-migration and from dissolution of households. That is, with a short history the population which can be sampled *ex post* resembles more closely the population that existed at the beginning of the prediction period.

New Departures

The models developed and tested here were based on assumption of equilibrium, at the time of entering any residence, between housing demand and housing consumption. The consumption equilibrium pattern itself, however, was never examined. Given housing cost and quality information, in addition to the data in the SHI on size and type of dwelling, it would be possible to investigate typical housing consumption by various types of families. Tradeoffs between size, quality, neighborhood characteristics, location, and cost at the time of a move, and the tradeoff between disequilibrium in current housing consumption and the cost of moving could be explored.

For these topics, too, additional data is required. In regard to housing costs, data on rent and value are basic. For owners it is also highly desirable to know fixed annual or monthly payments.[3] Age of structure, level of maintenance, and information on built-in features would be useful housing quality information. Built-in features to be recorded might include the number of baths, air conditioning and heating facilities, the number of floors in single-family houses, and elevators in multifamily. Data on such features could be used to derive an index of convenience or luxury.

Characteristics of the immediate surroundings are also important. Information of a simple type might be adequate. For example, in regard to land use, it might be enough to know which uses, identified in terms of a handful of categories, were found in the vicinity of the dwelling. Another important feature of the surroundings is the kind of street (e.g., local service, arterial) on which the housing faced. Average housing quality on a small area basis would also be helpful. In light of the high salience of race in the housing decisions of most families, racial occupancy patterns and shifts must be encompassed. Finally, the quality of public services should be considered. One study has shown measures of public school quality and of public safety to be significantly associated with a composite measure of residential blight.[4]

While the Penn Jersey Transportation Study did not develop usable data on cost and quality of individual housing units, it did collect information on many of the other topics listed above. Detailed land use and street classification data were standard items for a transportation study of that type. Other information is available from the 1960 U.S. Census. Thus, many aspects of housing choice, in addition to tenure, could be examined. Collating information from the Census and the several Penn Jersey files would not be easy, but it would be feasible. The rewards, in the form of research findings, might be substantial.

Although only the Penn Jersey files were mentioned above, by this time other metropolitan-area planning agencies might possess comparable data resources. It would be desirable to conduct comparative research on residential mobility and housing demand in a variety of metropolitan areas. Whatever agreement occurs among such studies will yield firmer findings, with broader scope, than can studies based on one urban area. Similarly, conflicting findings will pinpoint relationships that are either spurious or peculiar to one or a few areas. Either outcome would lead to better understanding of urban functioning.

Notes

Notes

Chapter 1
Introduction: The Symbiosis of
Mobility and Housing

1. Henry S. Shryock, Jr., *Population Mobility Within the United States* (Chicago: Community and Family Study Center, University of Chicago, 1964), Tables 5.1 and 5.2.

2. Shryock, Table 10.10.

3. William G. Grigsby, *Housing Markets and Public Policy* (Philadelphia: University of Pennsylvania Press, 1963), pp. 56-82; and Sherman J. Maisel, "Rates of Ownership, Mobility and Purchase," in *Essays in Urban Land Economics in Honor of the Sixty-Fifth Birthday of Leo Grebler* (Los Angeles: University of California, Real Estate Research Program, 1966).

4. Maisel, loc. cit.

5. V.V. Almendinger, "Topics in the Regional Growth Model: I" (Philadelphia: Penn Jersey Transportation Study, mimeographed, April 5, 1961), p. 5; and Gregory Ingram et al., *The NBER Urban Simulation Model: Volume I, The Model Description* (New York: National Bureau of Economic Research, no date).

6. See, for example, William Alonso, *Location and Land Use: Toward a General Theory of Land Rent* (Cambridge: Harvard University Press, 1965); J[ohn] R. Meyer, J[ohn] F. Kain, and M[artin] Wohl, *The Urban Transportation Problem*, Chapter 6 (Cambridge: Harvard University Press, 1965); and Ira S. Lowry, *Model of Metropolis*, Memorandum RM-4035-RC (Santa Monica: Rand Corporation, August 1964).

7. This problem has been analyzed with some success in relation to the WIN (Work Incentive) program, using Florida data that included work history after training. The paper in question is an unpublished master's research paper ("mini-thesis") in the Department of Urban and Regional Planning, The Florida State University, by James T. Clark, "Improving WIN Referrals in Florida" (1972).

Chapter 2
Perspectives on Mobility and Home
Purchase: A Review of the Literature

1. Melville C. Branch, Jr., *Urban Planning and Public Opinion: National Survey Research Investigation* (Princeton: Princeton University Press, 1942), p. 21.

2. Henry S. Shryock, Jr. and Elizabeth A. Larmon, "Some Longitudinal

Data on Internal Migration," *Demography*, 2:579-592 (1965). See Samuel Sabin, "Geographic Mobility and Employment Status March 1962–March 1963," *Monthly Labor Review*, 87:873-881 (August 1964), for a description of the survey on which Shryock and Larmon's article is based.

3. Vincent H. Whitney and Charles M. Brigg, "Patterns of Mobility Among a Group of Families of College Students," *American Sociological Review*, 23:643-652 (1958).

4. Sidney Goldstein and Kurt Mayer, "Migration and the Journey to Work," *Social Forces*, 42:472-481 (May 1964).

5. Nelson Foote et al., *Housing Choice and Housing Constraint* (New York: McGraw-Hill, 1960), pp. 153-158.

6. Sidney Goldstein and Kurt B. Mayer, *Residential Mobility, Migration and Commuting in Rhode Island* (Publication No. 7, Planning Division, Rhode Island Development Council, State Planning Section, September 1963), pp. 23-25.

7. Goldstein and Mayer found that in Warwick and Cranston, Rhode Island, two suburbs of Providence, half of the population that had moved in the period 1955-1960 had lived within the Providence suburban ring in 1955 (See *Residential Mobility . . .* , p. 10). Similarly, they found that three-fourths of the central city (Providence and Pawtucket) 1960 residents that had moved had lived in the central cities in 1955 (See *Residential Mobility . . .* , p. 9).

8. Michael A. Stegman, "Accessibility Models and Residential Location," *Journal of the American Institute of Planners*, 35:22-29 (1969). Stegman reports on the basis of a recent national survey that 27 percent of families moving between 1960 and 1966, stayed within the same neighborhood (not defined).

9. Theodore Caplow, "Incidence of and Direction of Residential Mobility in a Minneapolis Sample," *Social Forces*, 27:413-417 (1948-1949). Caplow's study of mobility within the city of Minneapolis included only families that had lived in the city for the entire period, 1940-1948. Of the families in his survey that satisfied the restraints, 55 percent remained in the same house, 66 percent in the same census tract, 74 percent approximately the same distance from city hall, and 82 percent in the same "section" of the city. That is, 27 percent of the respondents moved within the same "section" while 18 percent moved between "sections."

10. H. James Brown and John F. Kain, "Moving Behavior of San Francisco Households," Chapter 6 in John F. Kain, ed., *The NBER Urban Simulation Model: Volume II, Supporting Empirical Studies* (New York: National Bureau of Economic Research, no date).

11. Peter H. Rossi, *Why Families Move* (Glencoe, Illinois: Free Press, 1955) and Albert Chevan, *Moving in a Metropolitan Area* (unpublished Ph.D. dissertation, University of Pennsylvania, 1968).

12. Rossi, p. 74.

13. See Chevan, Table 45, p. 103.

14. Chevan, Tables 57 and 88, pages 119 and 157.

15. See, for example, Chevan, p. 102; Rossi, p. 69; and Foote et al., pp. 139-144.

16. Chevan, Tables 47 and 74, pp. 105 and 141.

17. Wendell Bell, "Social Choice, Life Styles, and Suburban Residence," in *The Suburban Community*, ed. by William M. Dobriner (New York: G.P. Putnam's Sons, 1958), pp. 225-247.

18. Ibid., p. 234.

19. Gerard R. Leslie, and Arthur H. Richardson, "Life Cycle, Career Patterns, and the Decision to Move," *American Sociological Review*, 26: 894-902 (1961).

20. Foote et al. suggest that sentiment and symbolic values contribute to the desire for home ownership (pp. 187-193). Research supporting a similar contention—that psychological and cultural factors contribute to the desire for ownership—is summarized in Glen H. Beyer, *Housing and Society* (New York: MacMillan Company, 1965), Chapter 7.

21. Chevan, Table 114, p. 197.

22. Ibid., p. 198.

23. Dorothy Swaine Thomas, *Research Memorandum on Migration Differentials* (New York: Social Science Research Council, Bulletin 43, 1938), p. 83.

24. Foote et al., pp. 149-153.

25. Sherman J. Maisel, "Rates of Ownership, Mobility and Purchase," in *Essays in Urban Land Economics in Honor of the Sixty-Fifth Birthday of Leo Grebler* (Los Angeles: University of California, Real Estate Research Program, 1966), pp. 76-108.

26. U.S. Department of Commerce, Bureau of the Census, *Current Population Reports*, Series P-20, No. 156, "Mobility of the Population of the United States, March, 1965—March, 1966" (1966), Table 2, p. 11.

27. Rossi, p. 42.

28. U.S. Bureau of the Census, loc. cit.

29. Ibid.

30. Henry S. Shryock, Jr., *Population Mobility Within the United States* (Chicago: Community and Family Study Center, University of Chicago, 1964), pp. 335-340.

31. Bruce C. Straits, "Residential Movement Among Negroes and Whites in Chicago," in Norval D. Glenn and Charles M. Bonjean, eds., *Blacks in the United States* (San Francisco: Chandler Publishing Company, 1969), pp. 114-133.

32. Ronald J. McAllister, Edward J. Kaiser, and Edward W. Butler, "Residential Mobility of Blacks and Whites: A National Longitudinal Survey," *American Journal of Sociology*, 77:445-456 (1971).

33. One of the better discussions of white response to the entrance of blacks is contained in Bruce C. Straits, "Racial Residential Succession" (unpublished paper prepared for the April, 1968, meeting of the Population Association of America, Boston). Whites with higher income, and whites who had lived longer

in the urban area (Chicago), tended to move out sooner than others when blacks entered a neighborhood.

34. Maisel, Table 2; also, Martin Heidenhain David, *Family Composition and Consumption* (Amsterdam: North Holland Publishing Company, 1962), Chapter 5.

35. Tong Hun Lee, "Demand for Housing: A Cross-Sectional Analysis," *Review of Economics and Statistics*, 45:190-196 (1963).

36. Chevan, pp. 104-105 and 141-142.

37. John F. Kain and John M. Quigley, "Housing Market Discrimination, Home Ownership, and Savings Behavior," *American Economic Review*, 62: 263-277 (1972).

38. The point has been illustrated in relation to the stock market, in Armen A. Alchian and William R. Allen, *University Economics*, Second Edition (Belmont, California: Wadsworth Publishing Company, 1967), pp. 89-91.

Chapter 3
Model of the Family Life Cycle and
Housing Decisions

1. Albert Chevan, *Moving in a Metropolitan Area* (unpublished Ph.D. dissertation, University of Pennsylvania, 1968).

2. John P. Shelton, "The Cost of Renting Versus Owning a Home," *Land Economics*, 44:59-72 (1968).

3. William Alonso, *Location and Land Use* (Cambridge: Harvard University Press, 1965).

4. Shelton, op. cit.

5. Nelson Foote, et al., *Housing Choice and Housing Constraint* (New York: McGraw-Hill, 1960), pp. 34-35; and Louis Winnick, *American Housing and its Use: The Demand for Shelter Space* (New York: John Wiley and Sons, Inc., 1957), pp. 44-48.

6. See Lewis G. Watts, et al., *The Middle Income Negro Faces Urban Renewal* (Waltham, Massachusetts: Brandeis University, Florence Heller Graduate School, Research Center, 1964); and Davis McEntire, *Residence and Race* (Berkeley and Los Angeles: University of California Press, 1960), pp. 238-250.

7. See L.K. Northwood and Ernest A.T. Barth, *Urban Desegregation: Negro Pioneers and Their White Neighbors* (Seattle: University of Washington Press, 1965).

8. Chester Rapkin and William G. Grigsby, *The Demand for Housing in Racially Mixed Areas* (Berkeley and Los Angeles: University of California Press, 1960), pp. 56-60.

9. Ronald G. Ridker, *Economic Costs of Air Pollution* (New York: Frederick A. Praeger, 1967), Chapter 6.

10. Chester Rapkin, "Price Discrimination against Negroes in the Rental Housing Market," in *Essays in Urban Land Economics in Honor of the Sixty-Fifth Birthday of Leo Grebler* (Los Angeles: University of California, Real Estate Research Program, 1966). Also, Beverly Duncan and Philip M. Hauser, *Housing a Metropolis–Chicago* (Glencoe, Illinois: Free Press, 1960), Chapter 6.

11. See McEntire, Chapter XI.

12. The effect of discrimination and supply restrictions on home ownership by blacks is given explicit empirical support in John F. Kain and John M. Quigley, "Housing Market Discrimination, Home Ownership, and Savings Behavior," *American Economic Review*, 62:263-277 (1972).

13. Chevan, p. 14.

14. Commission on Mortgage Interest Rates, *Report of the Commission on Mortgage Interest Rates to the President of the United States and to the Congress* (Washington, D.C.: Government Printing Office, August 1969), p. 26.

15. Commission on Mortgage Interest Rates, p. 3.

Chapter 4
Method of Investigation: A Problem
in Marginal and Contingent Probability

1. Guy H. Orcutt, et al., *Micro-Analysis of Socio-economic Systems: A Simulation Study* (New York: Harper and Brothers, 1961), Chapter 12. Orcutt, et al., examined the probability of a family's having mortgage debt, and the amount of debt, given that a mortgage debt is held.

2. Tong Hun Lee, "Demand for Housing: A Cross-Section Analysis," *Review of Economics and Statistics*, 45:190-196 (1963).

3. Sherman Maisel, "Rates of Ownership, Mobility and Purchase," in *Essays on Urban Land Economics in Honor of the Sixty-Fifth Birthday of Leo Grebler* (Los Angeles: University of California, Real Estate Research Program, 1966).

4. J. Johnston, *Econometric Methods* (New York: McGraw-Hill, 1963), pp. 221-228.

5. Stanley Leon Warner, *Stochastic Choice of Mode in Urban Travel* (Evanston: Northwestern University Press, 1962), p. 9.

6. See John P. Van de Geer, *Introduction to Multivariate Analysis for the Social Sciences* (San Francisco: W.H. Freeman and Company, 1971), Chapter 18.

7. R.A. Fisher, "The Statistical Utilization of Multiple Measurement," *Annals of Eugenics*, 8:376-386 (1937-1938). For an applied example and discussion, see Dwight M. Blood and C.B. Baker, "Some Problems of Linear Discrimination," *Journal of Farm Economics*, 40:674-683 (1958).

8. Discussion of the form and contents of the SHI is, unless otherwise noted, based upon unpublished material furnished by the Delaware Valley

Regional Planning Commission (the successor agency to the Penn Jersey Transportation Study) and conversations with Henry Bruck and Albert Chevan. Bruck and Chevan were responsible for conducting the SHI. A brief description of the SHI can be found in Penn Jersey Transportation Study, *PJ Report No. 1, Report on Study Procedures, Data Collection Phase* (Philadelphia: The Author, March 1961), pp. 14-16. Additional information can be found in Albert Chevan, *Moving in a Metropolitan Area* (unpublished Ph.D. dissertation, University of Pennsylvania, 1968), Chapter II, and in Albert Chevan, "Family Growth, Household Density and Moving," *Demography*, 8:451-458 (November 1971).

9. See Van de Geer, op. cit., pp. 250-251.

10. See George W. Ladd, "Linear Probability Analysis and Discriminant Functions," *Econometrica*, 34: 873-885 (1966).

11. Albert Chevan, op. cit., p. 18.

12. W. Lloyd Warner, Marcia Meeker, and Kenneth Eells, *Social Class in America: A Manual of Procedure for the Measurement of Social Class* (Chicago: Science Research Associates, Inc., 1949), Chapters 2, 8, and 9. Warner et al.'s classification scheme (pp. 140-141) was elaborated somewhat for use by Penn Jersey.

Chapter 5
Moving by the Married:
Empirical Analysis

1. U.S. Department of Commerce, Bureau of the Census, *U.S. Census of Population and Housing, 1960. Census Tracts.* Final Reports PHC (1)-116 and PHC (1)-160 (1962), Tables P-1, P-4 and—in report PHC (1)-116 only—P-5.

2. Paul C. Glick and Robert Parke, Jr., "New Approaches in Studying the Life Cycle of the Family," *Demography* 2:187-202 (1965).

3. Seymour Martin Lipset, *Social Mobility in Industrial Society* (Berkeley and Los Angeles: University of California Press, 1959), p. 174; and, U.S. Department of Labor, *Manpower Report of the President* (March 1964), pp. 138-139.

4. Gerard R. Leslie, and Arthur H. Richardson, "Life Cycle, Career Patterns, and the Decision to Move," *American Sociological Review*, 26:894-902 (1961). Leslie and Richardson did their research in an owner-occupied sub-division. (See Chapter 2 for further discussion.)

5. John P. Shelton, "The Cost of Renting Versus Owning a Home," *Land Economics*, 44:59-72 (1968).

6. J[ohn] R. Meyer, J[ohn] F. Kain and M[artin] Wohl, *The Urban Transportation Problem* (Cambridge: Harvard University Press, 1965), Chapter 6.

7. The test as used here is explained in J. Johnston, *Econometric Methods* (New York: McGraw-Hill Book Company, 1963), pp. 136-138.

8. H. James Brown and John F. Kain, "Moving Behavior of San Francisco Households," Chapter 6 in John F. Kain, ed. *The NBER Urban Simulation Model: Volume II, Supporting Empirical Studies* (New York: National Bureau of Economic Research, no date).

9. Peter H. Rossi, *Why Families Move* (Glencoe, Ill.: Free Press, 1955).

Chapter 7
The Decision to Buy or Rent

1. Nelson Foote et al., *Housing Choice and Housing Constraint* (New York: McGraw-Hill, 1960), pp. 34-35; and Louis Winnick, *American Housing and Its Use: The Demand for Shelter Space* (New York: John Wiley and Sons, Inc., 1957), pp. 44-48.

2. See Foote, et al., pp. 34-40, and Martin Heidenhain David, *Family Composition and Consumption* (Amsterdam: North Holland Publishing Company, 1962), Chapter 5.

Chapter 8
Summary, Conclusions, and Next Steps

1. V.V. Almendinger, "Topics in the Regional Growth Model: 1" (Philadelphia: Penn Jersey Transportation Study, mimeographed, April 5, 1961), p. 5; and Gregory Ingram, et al., *The NBER Urban Simulation Model: Volume I, The Model Description* (New York: National Bureau of Economic Research, no date).

2. See Institute of Urban Studies, University of Pennsylvania, *Industrial Land and Facilities for Philadelphia* (Philadelphia: Philadelphia City Planning Commission, 1956).

3. See Margaret G. Reid, *Housing and Income* (Chicago: University of Chicago Press, 1962), Chapter 3, for a discussion of the data that are typically available as against what would be desirable for housing consumption studies.

4. John F. Kain and John M. Quigley, "Evaluating the Quality of the Residential Environment," Discussion Paper No. 56, Program in Regional and Urban Economics, Harvard University (mimeographed, October 1969).

Bibliography

Bibliography

Alchian, Armen A., and Allen, William R. *University Economics*. 2nd ed. Belmont, California: Wadsworth Publishing Company, 1967.

Almendinger, V.V. "Topics in the Regional Growth Model: I." Philadelphia: Penn Jersey Transportation Study, April 5, 1961. (Mimeographed.)

Alonso, William. *Location and Land Use: Toward a General Theory of Land Rent*. Cambridge: Harvard University Press, 1965.

Bell, Wendell. "Social Choice, Life Styles, and Suburban Residence." *The Suburban Community*. Edited by William M. Dobriner. New York: G.P. Putnam's Sons, 1958.

Beyer, Glen H. *Housing and Society*. New York: Macmillan Company, 1965.

Blood, Dwight M.; and Baker, C.B. "Some Problems of Linear Discrimination." *Journal of Farm Economics*. 40:674-683 (1958).

Branch, Melville C., Jr. *Urban Planning and Public Opinion: National Survey Research Investigation*. Princeton: Princeton University Press, 1942.

Brown, H. James; and Kain, John F. "Moving Behavior of San Francisco Households." Chapter 6 in *The NBER Urban Simulation Model: Volume II, Supporting Empirical Studies*. Kain, John F., editor. New York: The National Bureau of Economic Research, no date.

Butler, Edgar W.; Chapin, F. Stuart, Jr.; Hemmens, George C.; Kaiser, Edward J.; Stegman, Michael A.; and Weiss, Shirley F. *Moving Behavior and Residential Choice: A National Survey*. National Cooperative Highway Research Program Report 81. Washington: Highway Research Board, 1969.

Butler, Edgar W.; and Kaiser, Edward J. "Predictions of Residential Movement and Spatial Allocation." *Urban Affairs Quarterly*. 6:477-494 (1970-1971).

Caplow, Theodore. "Incidence of and Direction of Residential Mobility in a Minneapolis Sample." *Social Forces*. 27:413-417 (1948-1949).

Carroll, J. Douglas, Jr. "Some Aspects of the Home-Work Relationships of Industrial Workers." *Land Economics*. 25:414-422 (1949).

Case, Fred E. *Cash Outlays and the Economic Costs of Home Ownership*. Los Angeles: University of California, Real Estate Research Program, 1957.

Chapin, F. Stuart, Jr. "Activity Systems as a Source of Inputs for Land Use Models." *Urban Development Models, Proceedings of a Conference Held June 26-30, 1967, Dartmouth College, Hanover, New Hampshire, HRB Special Report 97*. Washington: Highway Research Board, 1968, pp. 77-95.

Chevan, Albert. "Family Growth, Household Density, and Moving." *Demography*. 8:451-458 (November 1971).

Chevan, Albert. *Moving in a Metropolitan Area*. Unpublished Ph.D. dissertation, University of Pennsylvania, 1968.

Clark, James T. "Improving WIN Referrals in Florida." (Unpublished), 1972.

Commission on Mortgage Interest Rates. *Report of the Commission on Mortgage*

Interest Rates to the President of the United States and to the Congress. Washington, D.C.: Government Printing Office, August 1969.

David, Martin Heidenhain. *Family Composition and Consumption.* Amsterdam: North Holland Publishing Company, 1962.

Duncan, Beverly. "Factors in Work-Residence Separation: Wage and Salary Workers, Chicago, 1951." *American Sociological Review.* 21:48-56 (1956).

Duncan, Beverly, and Hauser, Philip M. *Housing a Metropolis—Chicago.* Glencoe, Illinois: Free Press, 1960.

Fava, Sylvia Fleis. "Suburbanism as a Way of Life." *American Sociological Review.* 21:34-37 (1956).

Federal Reserve Bulletin. 46 (1960).

Fisher, R.A. "The Statistical Utilization of Multiple Measurement." *Annals of Eugenics.* 8:376-386 (1937-1938).

Foote, Nelson; Abu-Lughod, Janet; Foley, Mary Mix; and Winnick, Louis. *Housing Choice and Housing Constraint.* New York: McGraw-Hill, 1960.

Glick, Paul C. *American Families.* New York: John Wiley and Sons, Inc., 1957.

Glick, Paul C. "Why Families Move." *American Sociological Review.* 12:164-174 (1947).

Glick, Paul C., and Parke, Robert, Jr. "New Approaches in Studying the Life Cycle of the Family." *Demography.* 2:187-202 (1965).

Goldstein, Sidney, and Mayer, Kurt B. "Migration and the Journey to Work." *Social Forces.* 42:472-481 (May 1964).

Goldstein, Sidney, and Mayer, Kurt B. *Residential Mobility, Migration and Commuting in Rhode Island.* Publication No. 7, Planning Division, Rhode Island Development Council, State Planning Section, September 1963.

Greenbie, Barrie Barstow. "New House or New Neighborhood? A Survey of Priorities among Home Owners in Madison, Wisconsin." *Land Economics.* 45:359-365 (August 1969).

Grigsby, William G. *Housing Markets and Public Policy.* Philadelphia: University of Pennsylvania Press, 1963.

Ingram, Gregory K.; Ginn, J. Royce; Brown, H. James; Kain, John F.; and Dresch, Stephen P. *The NBER Urban Simulation Model: Volume I, The Model Description.* New York: National Bureau of Economic Research, no date.

Institute of Urban Studies, University of Pennsylvania. *Industrial Land and Facilities for Philadelphia.* Philadelphia: Philadelphia City Planning Commission, 1956.

Johnston, J. *Econometric Methods.* New York: McGraw-Hill, 1963.

Kain, John F., and Quigley, John M. "Evaluating the Quality of the Residential Environment." Discussion Paper No. 56, Program in Regional and Urban Economics, Harvard University, October 1969. (Mimeographed.)

Kain, John F.; and Quigley, John M. "Housing Market Discrimination, Home Ownership, and Savings Behavior." *American Economic Review.* 62:263-277 (1972).

Katona, George; Lininger, Charles A.; and Kosobud, Richard F. *1962 Survey of Consumer Finance*. Ann Arbor, Michigan: The University of Michigan, Institute of Social Research, Survey Research Center, 1963.

Ladd, George W. "Linear Probability Analysis and Discriminant Functions." *Econometrica*, 34:873-885, 1966.

Lansing, John B.; Mueller, Eva; and Barth, Nancy. *Residential Location and Urban Mobility*. Ann Arbor: The University of Michigan, Institute for Social Research, Survey Research Center, 1964.

Lee, Tong Hun. "Demand for Housing: A Cross-Sectional Analysis." *Review of Economics and Statistics*. 45:190-196 (1963).

Leslie, Gerard R., and Richardson, Arthur H. "Life Cycle, Career Patterns, and the Decision to Move." *American Sociological Review*. 26:894-902 (1961).

Lind, Andrew W. "A Study of Mobility of Population in Seattle." *University of Washington Publications in Social Science*. Vol. 3, No. 1, pp. 1-64 (October 1925).

Lipset, Seymour Martin. *Social Mobility in Industrial Society*. Berkeley and Los Angeles: University of California Press, 1959.

Lowry, Ira S. *Model of Metropolis*, Memorandum RM-4035-RC. Santa Monica: Rand Corporation, August 1964.

Maisel, Sherman J. "Rates of Ownership, Mobility and Purchase." *Essays in Urban Land Economics in Honor of the Sixty-Fifth Birthday of Leo Grebler*. Los Angeles: University of California, Real Estate Research Program, 1966.

Marris, Peter. *Widows and Their Families*. London: Routledge and Kegan Paul, 1958.

McCallister, Ronald J.; Kaiser, Edward J.; and Butler, Edgar W. "Residential Mobility of Blacks and Whites: A National Longitudinal Survey." *American Journal of Sociology*, 77:445-456 (1971).

McEntire, Davis. *Residence and Race*. Berkeley and Los Angeles: University of California Press, 1960.

Meyer, J[ohn] R.; Kain, J[ohn] F.; and Wohl, M[artin]. *The Urban Transportation Problem*. Cambridge: Harvard University Press, 1965.

Moore, Eric G. "Comments on the Use of Ecological Models in the Study of Residential Mobility in the City." *Economic Geography*. 47:73-85 (1971).

_____. *Residential Mobility in the City*. Commission on College Geography Resource Paper No. 13. Washington: Association of American Geography, 1972.

Northwood, L.K., and Barth, Ernest A.T. *Urban Desegregation: Negro Pioneers and their White Neighbors*. Seattle: University of Washington Press, 1965.

Orcutt, Guy H.; Greenberger, Martin; Korbel, John; and Rivlin, Alice M. *Microanalysis of Socio-Economic Systems: A Simulation Study*. New York: Harper and Brothers, 1964.

Penn Jersey Transportation Study. PJ Report No. 1, *Report on Study Procedures, Data Collection Phase*. Philadelphia: The Author, March 1961.

Rapkin, Chester. "Price Discrimination against Negroes in the Rental Housing Market." *Essays in Urban Land Economics in Honor of the Sixty-Fifth Birthday of Leo Grebler*. Los Angeles: University of California, Real Estate Research Program, 1966.

Rapkin, Chester, and Grigsby, William G. *The Demand for Housing in Racially Mixed Areas*. Berkeley and Los Angeles: University of California Press, 1960.

Reid, Margaret G. *Housing and Income*. Chicago: University of Chicago Press, 1962.

Ridker, Ronald G. *Economic Costs of Air Pollution*. New York: Frederick A. Praeger, 1967.

Roseman, Curtis E. "Migration, the Journey to Work, and Household Characteristics: An Analysis Based on Non-Areal Aggregation." *Economic Geography*. 47:467-474 (1971).

Ross, H. Laurence. "Reasons for Moves to and from a Central City Area." *Social Forces*. 40:261-263 (1961-1962).

Rossi, Peter H. *Why Families Move*. Glencoe, Illinois: Free Press, 1955.

Sabagh, Georges; Van Arsdol, Maurice D., Jr.; and Butler, Edgar W. "Some Determinants of Metropolitan Residential Mobility: Conceptual Considerations," *Social Forces*. 48:88-98 (1969-1970).

Sabin, Samuel. "Geographic Mobility and Employment Status March 1962-March 1963." *Monthly Labor Review*. 87:873-881 (August 1964).

Shelton, John P. "The Cost of Renting Versus Owning a Home." *Land Economics*. 44:59-72 (1968).

Shryock, Henry S., Jr. *Population Mobility Within the United States*. Chicago: Community and Family Study Center, University of Chicago, 1964.

Shryock, Henry S., Jr., and Larmon, Elizabeth A. "Some Longitudinal Data on Internal Migration." *Demography*. 2:579-592 (1965).

Smith, Ruth H. "Housing Choices as Evidenced by Residential Mobility." *Journal of Home Economics*. 57:39-41 (1965).

Stegman, Michael A. "Accessibility Models and Residential Location." *Journal of The American Institute of Planners*. 35:22-29 (1969).

Straits, Bruce C. "Racial Residential Succession." Unpublished paper prepared for the April, 1968, meeting of the Population Association of America, Boston. (Mimeographed.)

Straits, Bruce C. "Residential Movement Among Negroes and Whites in Chicago." In Norval D. Glenn and Charles M. Bonjean, eds. *Blacks in the United States*. San Francisco: Chandler Publishing Company, 1969, pp. 114-133.

Taeuber, Karl E., and Taeuber, Alma F. "White Migration and Socio-Economic Differences between City and Suburbs." *American Sociological Review*. 29:718-729 (1964).

Thomas, Dorothy Swaine. *Research Memorandum on Migration Differentials*. New York: Social Science Research Council, Bulletin 43, 1938.

U.S. Department of Commerce, Bureau of the Census. *Current Population*

Reports, Series P-20, No. 156, "Mobility of the Population of the United States, March 1965–March 1966." (1966).

U.S. Department of Commerce, Bureau of the Census. *Statistical Abstract of the United States: 1968* (89th Edition).

U.S. Department of Commerce, Bureau of the Census. *U.S. Census of Population and Housing, 1960. Census Tracts*. Final Reports PHC (1)-116, Philadelphia, Pa.-N.J., and PHC (1)-160, Trenton, N.J. (1962).

U.S. Department of Labor. *Manpower Report of the President*. March 1964.

Van de Geer, John P. *Introduction to Multivariate Analysis for the Social Sciences*. San Francisco: W.H. Freeman and Company, 1971.

Warner, Stanley Leon. *Stochastic Choice of Mode in Urban Travel*. Evanston: Northwestern University Press, 1962.

Warner, W. Lloyd; Meeker, Marcia; and Eells, Kenneth. *Social Class in America: A Manual of Procedure for the Measurement of Social Class*. Chicago: Science Research Associates, Inc., 1949.

Watts, Lewis G.; Freeman, Howard E.; Hughes, Helen M.; Morris, Robert; and Pettigrew, Thomas F. *The Middle-Income Negro Family Faces Urban Renewal*. Waltham, Mass.: Brandeis University, Florence Heller Graduate School, Research Center, 1964.

Whitney, Vincent H., and Brigg, Charles M. "Patterns of Mobility Among a Group of Families of College Students." *American Sociological Review*. 23:643-652 (1958).

Winnick, Louis. *American Housing and its Use: The Demand for Shelter Space*. New York: John Wiley and Sons, Inc., 1957.

Index

About the Author

Daniel R. Fredland has been teaching Urban and Regional Planning at Florida State University since 1970. He received the Ph.D. from Harvard University and the M.C.P. from the University of Pennsylvania. Prior to Ph.D. studies, he spent several years as a practicing planner with The Planning Services Group Inc., of Cambridge, Massachusetts and the Penn Jersey Transportation Study (now Delaware Valley Regional Planning Commission). His interest in analyzing urban location patterns and their causes and effects is long-standing. It began with his experiences during summer college recesses as a planning assistant at the Detroit Metropolitan Area Regional Planning Commission. It has continued since then to be a major focus of his work.